Frank's War

Thornycroft

(An Army Service Corps Diary)

By Brian (Harry) Clacy

Dedication

This book is dedicated to every professional truck driving soldier of the British Army, both past and present, and regardless of which Corps name they served under. From the Royal Waggoners right up to the Royal Logistic Corps, as far as I am concerned they are all Trog's/Trogg's regardless of the spelling.

Definition of a Trog/Trogg: Any truck driving soldier who has proudly served within the ranks of the Royal Corps of Transport.

Brian (Harry) Clacy

Ancestry of British Army Transport Formations

The Royal Waggoners 1794 – 1795

The Royal Waggon Train 1799 – 1833

Land Transport Corps 1855 – 1857

The Military Train 1857 – 1869

Army Service Corps 1869 – 1881

Commissariat and Transport Corps 1881 – 1886

Army Service Corps 1889 – 1918

Royal Army Service Corps 1918 – 1965

Royal Corps of Transport 1965 – 1993

Royal Logistic Corps 1993 - to date

Acknowledgements

Without Steve Parsons this story would never have been told. The likelihood is that Frank Sanderson's medals and diaries would probably have remained undiscovered for another one hundred years. I am honoured that Steve gave me the chance to write this story about his Step-Grandfather and that my friend Stevie Johnson recommended me for the task, writing this book has been a labour of love.

Terry Cavender, Colin Booth, and Ken Baines have made my task a lot easier than it should have been, I am eternally indebted to the three of you for your proof reading, research and technical advice. Many thanks must also go to the National Archives, the Carnegie Heritage Centre in Hull, and members of the Facebook site, 'Hull the Good Old Days'.

Father Andrew Howard and George Armitage (PCC Secretary) of St Wilfrids Church, in Doncaster actually found the site of Frank's grave for Steve Parsons, they also researched the Parish Burial Details to confirm where and when he was laid to rest. Father Howard and George Armitage were both present when we laid a poppy wreath on Frank's headstone and said a simple prayer. Rest In Peace Frank, your duty is done.

My own son Matthew has proof read this book for me and he's also given me much encouragement and advice, many thanks son.

The fantastic cover for this book was designed and produced by Eric Hartley BA MA (Hons) and Reece Taylor of ELK marketing in Beverley East Yorkshire, it was Eric's idea to use a cream border to make the book cover look similar to the military recruiting posters used during the First World War. ELK Marketing have come up trumps again.

My very talented friend Robert Darkin designed and painted the drawing of an ASC driver on page 3, Bob has rather cleverly drawn the picture in a similar style to the artwork of Bruce Bairnsfather. He also did a fantastic job on refurbishing Frank's medals. Top job mate.

Those of you who have read my other books know I always give an acknowledgement to my beautiful and long-suffering wife Nicky Clacy, Nicky has helped me transcribe Frank's diaries, she's also drawn the pictures of vehicles for the book and helped me with all of my techno-phobic problems with this bloody laptop and the tintinet. Again, I owe you so much Nicky, and all you get in return is my undying love and devotion...that and the occasional fairly decent home-made Lamb Rogan Josh curry.

Lastly, I would like to thank Private Frank Sanderson ASC for writing his wonderful diaries in the first place and for giving our nation a very rare insight into the life of an Army Service Corps drivers experiences during the Great War. Frank was a soldier who went to war in a Thornycroft lorry.

Brian (Harry) Clacy

Introduction

Many books have been written by countless authors about the First World War. Each book contains a valuable and informative historical record of virtually every aspect of the Great War on Land, Sea, and in the Air. We suppose that the PBI (Poor Bloody Infantry) suffered more than most because they both lived and died in the Front Line Trenches every single day from 1914 until 1918. They were shot at by snipers, shelled by the Artillery, were burned alive by flame-throwers, suffered from Trench Foot, Hypothermia, Frost Bite and were constantly plagued with body lice, and during the summer months they suffered from de-hydration and heat stroke because of the problems getting fresh water up to soldiers on all of the front lines.

As if these incessantly dangerous and desperate living conditions weren't bad enough, in 1915 the Germans added poison gas into their already vast and devastating armoury. Blister, Phosgene and Chlorine agents not only incapacitated soldiers by blinding, blistering and choking them, the gasses often proved to be lethal, only too often after many years of suffering by the casualties. Some of the victims taking many years to die from lung diseases and cancers caused by the toxic chemicals. According to the Imperial War Museum there were roughly 600,000 First World War pensions still being paid out 11 years after the war had ceased, only 1% of these were gas casualties.

Over the years I have read a vast amount of books about the First World War by such illustrious authors as Lyn MacDonald, Richard Holmes, Malcolm Brown, Jeremy Paxman and Anthony Babington. I have read about most 'Great War' subjects ranging from the First World War's medical services, the touchy subject of executing soldiers for cowardice, the perceived romantic images of the Christmas truce at Ploegstreert in 1914, and even about T. E. Lawrence's post-war experiences in the Royal Air Force in his posthumously published book entitled, 'The Mint.' 'The War the Infantry Knew 1914-1919' was written by Captain J C Dunn DSO, MC and Bar, DCM. This huge hard-backed manuscript gives a fantastic perception of what an RAMC doctor experienced in the front-line whilst serving with an Infantry Battalion, it's yet another great document about this wretched war. Books about the other side of the divide are also great reading. Stephen Westerman's 'Surgeon with the Kaiser's Army' and Ernst Junger's 'Storm of Steel' (Ernst was a Storm Trooper in the same German Army) give the German's view of the catastrophe. The German subjects on the war are very similar to most of the allied versions; they're mostly about the fighting and medical elements of their army. All of these and many others are fantastic books to read and they deserve the many plaudits already received. From the books I've already mentioned one gets a sense of what subjects most military authors like to write about, and what their readers are channelled into reading.

I would like to put one question to all you aficionados' of military reading. How many First World War books have you read that cover the personal experiences of 'behind the lines' soldiers? Not many I'll bet. You might have read Captain James Agate's communiques in, 'Lines of Communication,' or Sergeant T Secrett's autobiography, 'Twenty-five years with Earl Haig.' I'll put good money on the fact that there aren't many other First World War 'Rank and File', rear echelon, personal biographies that you could name. Most books written about the Great War are written by Officers because, prior to 1914, if you hadn't been to Eton, Cambridge or Oxford, then you were lucky if you could string two words together on a chalk board. One of my favourite Officer books is by the obsequious and toadying Brigadier-General John Charteris, in my opinion, his book 'Field-Marshal Earl Haig' is simply just another boring and impersonal 'Officer Style' documentary that isn't exactly noteworthy.

Another reason for a lack of 'Rank and File' books could be that in 1919 every man jack was simply fed up with the war, everyone, which includes those who hadn't served, had seen enough of death and suffering and they just wanted to forget about what they'd all been through. The British Nation was looking forward to a wonderful future in a 'Land Fit for Heroes' as promised by David Lloyd George's government. If people were going to read anything about the war it would have to be stories of courage, derring-do and what it was like to battle hand-to-hand and face-to-face with the enemy. Stories about the Army Service Corps would probably come well down any readers' wish-list, certainly after tales about the Royal Flying Corps, the Machine-gun Corps and the Royal Navy at the Battle of Jutland. I personally have read many of these types of books and yet the War Diaries of a Private serving in the Army Service Corps, has probably been the most fascinating personal account I've ever read. Mainly because of its simplicity and the fact that it isn't what could be referred to as 'main-stream'.

On the evening of Saturday 23rd January 2016, Mr Stephen Parsons telephoned me from his home in Doncaster, he'd been speaking to an old army friend of mine called Stevie Johnson. In his heyday Stevie was an extraordinary and well respected army boxer who had served in the Royal Corps of Transport. Over a pint at their local club Stephen explained that he'd found his Step-Grandfathers First World War diaries and medals in his attic. He wasn't sure what to do with them and because Stevie Johnson had been a soldier, he asked him for some advice because it seemed such a shame to just leave them gathering dust in his house. Stevie Johnson gave him my home telephone number and told him to contact me. I'm honoured that Stevie Johnson told him, "Harry's an author and will probably write a book about them, and I can assure you he'll do a great job." I drove over to Doncaster to pick up the diaries and medals and later that day my wife Nicky and I started transcribing them word for word exactly how they'd been written. I have even included the spelling mistakes and written the diary entries precisely how they were laid out in both notebooks. I was so excited to hold and read these personal records that had been written on the Western Front 100 years previously. Some of the details are quite mundane, such as this entry Frank made on the 20th of August 1915: "Parades & usual work. A very wet day. 4th pay day receiving 40 francs." Other entries tell us exactly what sort of military equipment he was issued at his Depot in Grove Park South London before starting his Basic Training. We are also told, word for word, what he had for Christmas dinner whilst based at Marles-le-Mines near Bethune in December 1915. The diaries describe which type of vehicle Frank was driving on a given day and what duties he carried out whilst driving for 282 Company ASC (Army Service Corps). Frank's Company was operating in support of 13th and 15th Siege Batteries RGA (Royal Garrison Artillery).

To help me write this book I have visited the National Archives at Kew in London and have downloaded the War Diaries of each unit that Frank had served within. As an ex-soldier and author, they make fascinating reading. Sadly, the majority of these notes probably won't be read or used ever again, but they were written by Officers at the time of, or shortly after, yet another Western Front battle. These hand written summaries are an actual record of a time in our military history and although maybe not as, supposedly, stimulating as those of other notable soldiers like Field Marshal Haig, they are very interesting nonetheless.

The following entry was written by Captain Pilkington ASC who was attached to an R.G.A Ammunition Column. The Unit War Diary gives a brief insight into the incredibly dangerous and hard work that was carried out by drivers of the Army Service Corps:

"Each of the batteries had what was called a 'Roving Gun.' This was taken up, after dark to a very forward position (which was almost always under mustard-gas shell fire) where anything up to 100 rounds were fired, it was then returned to its rear position before daylight. Altogether these were most trying moves. Whilst at Houthem Cpl (*Corporal*) Hogg and L/cpl (*Lance Corporal*) Boughton were awarded the Military Medal for saving several loaded lorries parked together which, struck by a shell caught fire. Other Rank casualties: Killed – 3 Wounded – 9 Gassed – 2."

Everything you read in this book has been transcribed from Frank's diaries, exactly as Frank wrote them. Anything in italic bold, (like the above ranks), are my own notes that are included simply to clarify things for you the reader. Unlike a lot of Private soldiers in the First World War, Frank was obviously an intelligent and well educated young man because the diaries are, in the main, beautifully written in fountain pen with very few spelling, punctuation, or grammatical errors. When he wrote his entries he always used an ampersand "&" rather than using the full word 'and', in fact I think he only used the word "and" once in all of his notes.

Before we get to the meat of the diaries, I'd like to give you the reader an understanding of the Corps in which Frank was serving during the Great War. At the height of its heyday during World War One, the Army Service Corps was the largest military formation in the British Army. It had a complement of over 10,000 Officers and 300,000 soldiers who served in a myriad of trades. The list of jobs that soldiers of the Army Service Corps covered goes some way into highlighting why it was such a massive organisation. The Corps provided Butchers, Bakers, Ambulance Drivers, Railwaymen, Clerks, Mechanics, Storemen, Lorry Drivers, Dispatch Riders, Foragers, Blacksmith's and it even provided the drivers for the Worlds very first tank battle at Flers-Courcellette in 1916. These duties were carried out every day of the war and if they weren't done properly and efficiently, then the mighty wheels of the British Army would simply have stopped turning. Infantrymen can't fight a war without ammunition and food. And yet the Army Service Corps was much maligned by the fighting troops who believed that the 'jam stealing' drivers had a cushy time behind the lines and so they referred to the Army Service Corps as, 'Anglais San Courage', which is French for, 'the English without courage'.

The ASC not only had to source and provide the British Army with all of its day to day necessities, but it also had to get these items from where they were produced and right up to the front lines on the Western, Eastern, Balkan, Mesopotamian (including Gallipoli) and Palestine fronts. To transport these stores the ASC used ships, trains, horses, barges, and of course an excess of lorries, caterpillar tractors, motor-cycles, staff cars and omnibuses. The British Army was the first ever fully motorised fighting force the world had seen and M2/081323 Private Frank Sanderson ASC was just one small cog in its gigantic organisational wheel. You'll see when you read this book that Frank made an entry into his diary every single day (he was just 20 years old when he started writing in the first notebook), his last being made on the 12th of January 1917. There were a lot of things going on in the world whilst Frank was on the Western Front, and he was right there in the thick of some of it.

Here is a sample of just some of those principal events that happened during Frank's time in France and some of which are mentioned in his diaries:

29 January 1914. Paris was bombed by German Zeppelins for the first time.

21 February 1916. Start of the Battle of Verdun.

27 April 1916. Over two days the German Army used their most heavily-concentrated gas attack of the war, 47th Brigade, 16th Irish Division was decimated.

1 July 1916. First day of the Battle of the Somme.

14 July 1916. The Battle of Bazentin Ridge begins which signifies the start of Phase Two of the Battle of the Somme.

15 September 1916. The Battle of Flers-Courcelette begins and this attack was the first time tanks had been used in modern war-fare. The tanks were driven by Army Service Corps drivers who eventually transferred into the Royal Tank Corps on 28th July 1917.

28 September 1916. British and French Troops finally take and hold Thiepval Ridge and the Schwaben Redoubt.

13 November 1916. Foch and Haig launch the Battle of Ancre which was the final attack by British and French soldiers during the Battle of the Somme.

18 November 1916. The Battle of the Somme ends.

18 December 1916. The Battle of Verdun ends.

This is just a segment of some of Frank's observations in his diaries, the personal thoughts of a down to earth young army lorry driver from Hull, and how he simply, but effectively, described what happened in his small part of the world's history, whilst 'hell on earth' swirled on around him.

Brian (Harry) Clacy

'1915'

'The war diaries of Private Frank Sanderson Army Service Corps'

23rd April 1915. Reading the advertisements in the local paper of that date, I noticed motor-drivers were wanted for the British Army; so I decided to offer my services to the country. I proceeded to the City Hall (**Hull**) & was accepted after passing the doctor. My orders were to report on Thursday the 29th.

29th Called at City Hall, & was examined before Lieutenant Gardiner & was accepted; afterwards being sworn in along with 6 others by Alderman Crook. I consider in doing this I executed my duty, satisfied my own conscience, & pleased my friends.

30th This was the last day with my employers & the last in the city. (***Frank was working as a Leaded Light Maker before enlisting, his job would have involved him working on the construction of domestic coloured glass designs used in front doors and stairwell windows.***)

1st May 1915 Mobilised at City Hall 10 am & was given passes to proceed by rail to A.S.C. depot at Lee (***in***) London & I left the Hall at 11.30 am & marched to Paragon station taking the 11.45 am express to King's Cross. Arrived Kings Cross about 5.30 pm. Before starting on the journey we were paid 14/- (***Shillings***) each (***£72.86p in today's money***). Took the tube from King's Cross to Cannon St & then went by SE & C Rly to Lee (***An Army Service Corps Reception and Training Depot.***) arriving at the station at 7.30 pm.

Leaving the station at 7.30 pm we received a most sympathetic reception from the A.S.C. recruits stationed there, one which I shall ever remember. (***Banter between recruits and seasoned soldiers has always been a popular sport within the British Army.***) Proceeded to the depot of the M.T. (***Motor***

Transport) A.S.C. which was a workhouse (Grove Park Workhouse). Handed my attestation papers to N.C.O. in charge. Here I had the misfortune to be separated from my mate Johnnie. I was told off to E Company & he was sent to C Company. Afterwards we were served out with 2 blankets each, & put in what was the dining room for the night. (***Grove Park was just one of many ASC Training Establishments in the South of England. The building at Grove Park in South East London was requisitioned as an ASC Depot in September 1914 about one month after Britain declared war on Germany. At Grove Park the Army Service Corps NCO instructors turned recruits into soldiers and 100 London General Omnibus Company bus drivers, turned those soldiers into MT drivers.***)

2nd A most uncomfortable night it was too. About 40 men were in the room & some slept on the tables, others on the forms, while the rest had to take the floor. All had a bad night, for it was dreadfully cold & clocks of beetles were crawling about all over. Woke up about 4 a.m. & dressed. Walked around the barracks while 7 oclock & then paraded for breakfast, which I obtained after a long wait in the corridors, consisting of a basin of tea & bread & butter & cold ham. Hung about while after dinner, which consisted of potatoes & mutton & an apple for dessert.

Afterwards we were served out with our equipment. Greatcoat, tunic, trousers, boots, puttees, 3 pair socks, 2 pair pants, 1 vest, belt & pouches, cap, jack-knife, water-bottle, haversack, house-wife, hold-all, kitbag, razor, knife, fork & spoon, comb, toothbrush & shaving brush, Jersey, braces, cap-comforter, rifle (an old cavalry carbine No 11097), 2 shirts, 1 towel, 2 blankets, billy can & cover. Went in the open yard & changed into uniform & packed other clothes up & forwarded home. Afterwards we had tea & then took a walk into Lee. The 2nd night we slept at Lynduru (***presumably this was the name of the house in which he was accommodated.***) in an empty house close to the barracks. (***It has been recorded that civilians in Grove Park often commented on the Army Service Corps drivers dress at the time, it was mentioned that the drivers had initially appeared quite scruffy. Tunics were oversized, trousers were too short, and their hats kept falling off their heads because they were too small, others complained they couldn't see where they were going because the even larger hats covered the soldier's eyes and made*** their ears stick out. *Most Quartermaster departments at the time had a "One size fits all" policy.*)

3rd Revellie 6 a.m. Breakfast 7.30. Dinner 12.30. Tea 4.30. was the proceedings of the day. In the afternoon we were moved to an empty house close to Grove Park Station. This was termed No 1 Billet. (*No 1 Billet was a large double fronted and detached house, it had bay windows on the ground floor and the path that led up to the porched front door cut through a very smart garden. The large tree positioned on the pavement to the side of the house intimated that No 1 Billet must have been owned by an affluent Edwardian family.*)

4th Proceedings as usual for the day. Called on to do guard for 24 hours. My 1st experience of the duty which was 2 hours on & 4 off. J Chamberlain was my companion on guard.

5th Marched from No 1 Billet to Barracks & issued out with identification disc & pay-book. Took my number 081329. (*On official documentation Frank's service number would have been recorded as M2/081329, the M denoted he was a Motor Transport driver, the difference between an M1 and M2 driver remains unclear even today. One theory states that M2 drivers weren't Regular Army soldiers but those who had enlisted after the start of the First World War.*)

6th Marched from billet to Barracks at 1 p.m. & proceeded by motor-bus from there to Camberwell where 10 Thornycroft lorries were taken over. Then we went along to Peckham & from there 20 Peerless lorries were taken over. W Redpath & myself took over a Peerless. All these lorries were driven back to the depot & were lined up on the side of the road going to Nottingham from Grove Park. This was our 1st night sleeping in the lorries, which we have made our homes & fitted out as comfortable as possible. Number of lorry 4825C. (*Thornycroft was a UK based manufacturer that provided vehicles for the British Army from 1902 onwards, in 1901 vehicle selection trials were held in Aldershot to decide which firm should be awarded a vehicle supply contract* to the British Army. The Thornycroft steam lorry won first prize, Foden came second and the Straker vehicle came third. Lord Kitchener wrote in his post-trials report, "Thornycroft's are the best" and so it was the Thornycroft's that saw service in the Boer War. The same firm was still providing vehicles for the British Army, and in particular, the Royal Corps of Transport, up until the 1980's when the Mighty Antar Tank Transporter was in its heyday.)

THORNYCROFT

7th Was put through our first drill by Serg (***Sergeant***) Hughes & Corp (***Corporal***) Fowles. This also was our first pay day in the army. We paraded at Barracks & was paid in alphabetical order. My first pay was £1. (***In today's valuation £1 in 1915 would equate to £104.08p.***)

8th Drill at 10.30 till 11.30 a.m. After tea took a quiet walk into Lee. On the way we bought cap and shoulder badges. (***Brass accoutrements like these were always paid for out of a soldiers own pay and by doing this the War Department must have saved itself a considerable amount of expenditure.***)

9th This was our 2nd Sunday in the forces. A quiet day was spent. In the evening W. Redpath & myself took train from Grove Park to Bromley Kent. Formed a very nice opinion of the town so returned to the station, only to find we had missed the train so set off & walked home a distance of 4 miles.

10th Went with a Thornycroft lorry to the A.S.C. stores London for stores for the Company. Arrived back about 2 p.m. (*The Army Service Corps' driver training increased the Grove Park traffic by at least ten-fold, and the local council complained to the War Department about the damage sustained to their roads. The Thornycroft's were a 3 ton petrol and chain driven lorry that had a maximum speed of 12 mph. It was used as a General Service vehicle for moving troops, ammunition, petrol, rations, Royal Engineer equipment, and it was even used in the anti-aircraft role by having a large howitzer bolted onto its cargo area, extending stabilisation legs were fitted underneath and these were deployed before the weapon was fired.*)

11th Drill as usual. Fire extinguisher served out to each lorry. (*In 1914 a US Company called Pyrene produced hand pumped brass fire extinguishers for the War Department, the extinguishers were manufactured under licence in the UK.*) Had a trial run with the lorries of about 5 miles. Had a photo taken of the lorry. A grand concert was held in the large dining hall at the Barracks this night, was very much enjoyed by us all. This was the last time I was with Johnnie & have never come across him since. My second time on guard, but with rifle this time.

12th Drill as usual. Visited the soldier's institute at Grove Park & wrote several letters. A very nice place & much appreciated by the troops. (*The Soldier's Institute was similar to other Christian clubs like the YMCA and Talbot House. It was a religious house of sanctuary for off-duty servicemen where they could get away from the army for a while, they could buy a cup of tea and read a newspaper in peace and quiet, and they could also have an ecclesiastical shoulder to cry on if necessary.*)

13th A very wet day & was compelled to stay in our lorries for shelter. This was our last day at the depot. We were all anxious to get on the move & everyone was desirous of getting to the front. You can imagine after 11 days at the depot we were getting nicely into our new life. We had much to put up with & all missed the little comforts of civilian life. The food was good, but there was no variety & not cooked as we had been used to having it. Shaving was a fearful duty. Seeing we had to use cold water, you can imagine what terrible faces there was before breakfast every morning. About 4 oclock in the afternoon our C.O. (**Commanding Officer**), Lieu (**Lieutenant**) Young gave us orders to prepare for moving at once. About 30 extra men with Serg Major's (**Sergeant-Major's**) Fisher and Harrison joined us on this date. By 5 oclock all cars were ready & we were on our way to somewhere, all being pleased to see the last of Grove Park. The weather was most terrible, & we stayed in Staines (**Another ASC camp**) for the night. After arrival we were served out with water-proof-sheets which were very acceptable for everyone concerned.

14th Left Staines at 8 a.m. & proceeded to Basingstoke, where we stopped in the main street & were served out with dinner. On that occasion it was dry bread and cheese. From there we went along to Salisbury over the Plain, where we partook of tea which we had to provide ourselves. Leaving Salisbury at 5 p.m. we arrived at Blandford about 8 p.m. (**At this stage of the war Blandford Camp was being used as a depot for soldiers of the RND (Royal Naval Division), these surplus to requirement sailors were trained as Infantrymen to boost the under-manned ranks of the British Army's fighting soldiers.**)

15th Left Blandford at 8 a.m. & proceeded to Taunton, via Yeovil & arrived at our destination about 2 p.m. Here we were attached to the 19th Siege Battery, Royal Garrison Artillery, under the command of Major Moberly. Having had nothing since breakfast, the garrison boys knowing we were coming, we had a good dinner awaiting us in the barracks. These are very nice barracks & we were all very comfortable during the 7 days we stayed there. We were provided with straw mattresses & pillows here & it was quite a treat to retire for the night. (**From the early 1960's the towns of Yeovil and Taunton became Training establishments for the Royal Army Service Corps and Royal Corps of Transport, the two Corps that succeeded the Army Service Corps.**)

16th Paraded on the drill field used by the R.G.A (Royal Garrison Artillery) at 10 a.m. & was put through our drills by Serg (*Sergeant*) Harrison. In the evening we took a walk around Taunton. It is a very nice little town & the people are very sociable.

17th Paraded at 1030 a.m. & inspected by Major Moberly. Drill as usual. In the afternoon we received our pay.

18th Drill as usual in the morning. In the afternoon about half of the men of the A.S.C. were inoculated, myself included. (*In 1914 Rabies, Typhoid, and Tetanus Toxoid vaccines had already been developed and Frank could have been injected with all or some of these.*)

19th Being inoculated we received 48 hours leave. This was very acceptable for it affected most of the men & rest was very welcome. (*Prior to the recent Wars in Iraq, many soldiers were given a cocktail of vaccinations and they also had to be bedded down for 24/48 hours. Some aspects in the life of a soldier never change.*) A nice reading room in the barracks was well patronised. There was a Y.M.C.A (*Young Men's Christian Association*) in the town, also a Soldiers Home (*another Christian Club*) and both were very convenient to the troops.

20th Our sick leave having finished in the afternoon, we were ready for work again. To our surprise we were paid again in the afternoon, much to our benefit for everyone can do with 2 pay days per week.

21st There was a general sorting out on this day. The best men were chosen to remain with the battery, also the best lorries were retained. About 30 men & 12 Peerless lorries were sent back to Bulford camp under Serg Maj (*Sergeant Major*) Harrison's command. W. Redpath, (my mate), and myself here got separated. He was placed on a store lorry (a Peerless), & proceeded with 6 other lorries along with the 2 (*two*) 8" (*inch*) Howitzers & 2 Catterpillars

(*Caterpillars*) to Highbridge on the way to Bristol. On this day Italy declared war on Austria. I was placed on a Peerless along with A. Swingler on this day & along with a Thornycroft, we were ordered to remain behind & wait for stores. LcCorp (*Lance Corporal*) Richardson had charge of these 2 lorries. (*The Peerless Lorry was an American truck that was developed, produced and exported from Cleveland Ohio, from 1915 until the end of the war in 1918, the British Government bought over 12,000 of them for use by the British Army. The Peerless was a heavy and robust lorry with a four speed gear-box and it was propelled by a rear-wheel chain drive that was very slow by today's standards. It could only manage a restricted 16 mph.*)

22nd The stores not having come we had practically nothing to do. The remaining cars in the column were attached to the left half of the battery & stayed in Taunton a week longer than the others of the right half to which we were attached. (My first opportunity to wash my underclothing). (*Yuk!*)

23rd The stores having come, we left Taunton about 10 a.m. for Bristol. Was sorry to leave Taunton for we spent an enjoyable time there. We reached Bristol about 1 p.m. having come via Highbridge, and Redhill. Making a mistake we passed our stopping place & got right down to Avonmouth Docks & seeing none of our Company we turned back & met the despatch rider who was seeking us. We joined the rest of the right half battery who were stationed in the Artillery Ground in Whiteladies Road. Here we were billeted in houses & were most comfortable. It was like being back at home. I stayed in a very nice resturant (*restaurant*) & we were made so comfortable. It was about 1 minutes walk from the Downs which is one of Bristol's noted places. In the evening we took a walk round the town. (*A lot of troops and vehicles arrived and departed from Bristol's Avonmouth Docks during the First World War.*)

24th This was Bank Holiday. Cars were attended to & all preparations made for the following day. Here A. Swindler was taken off my car being only a poor driver & P. Macgregor was put in his place & has been my mate since then. A great recruiting route took place in Bristol to-day. In the afternoon Major Moberly gave us a very interesting lecture about the 19th Siege Battery. In the evening we had an enjoyable time in Bristol, along with J.W.Shaw.

25th The lorries proceeded to Avon-mouth at 7.30 & were put on board one of H.M. Ship's Transport's. The remainder of the men had to stay one more day in the town. With the holiday, there were several eligible young men walking about & several of us did our best amongst us in obtaining recruits. Several came forward & J. W. Shaw did much in securing them. In the afternoon Corporal Burton gave us a lecture on the rifle. In the evening we again had a good time in the town.

26th Paraded in the field at 7.30 a.m. and marched behind the R.G.A (*Royal Garrison Artillery*) men to Stapletown Rd station. A most awful march it was too. A terribly hot morning, & full kit, I got my baptism of a route march. This was a distance of 4 miles. We left the town about 9 a.m. & proceeded by train to Southampton, via Bath & Salisbury on the G. W. Rly (*Great Western Railway*). Arrived at the docks at 12 noon & had a dinner consisting of biscuits and bully beef. This was our first trial of the biscuits & a most dis-heartening one too. More than one broke their false teeth with them so you can imagine how hard they were. Tea was served out on the docks & biscuits were again the staff of life along with jam. (*Hardtack biscuits were originally designed for the Royal Navy and were simply made of flour, water and salt, manufacturers sometimes baked them up to four times and the biscuits were so solid that they could be stored for years before being eaten. Ideal for a long sea voyage. It has been documented many times that First World War soldiers with dentures often broke their false teeth when trying to eat them dry. The best way to consume them was to crumble the crackers into a stew or just soaking them in a mug of hot sweet tea until they softened.*)

While on the docks we met a number of Indian soldiers. We all formed a very good opinion of them & they crossed the channel by the same boat as did our battery. They were returning to the front after recovering from wounds whilst in action. Since then we have met with several whilst out here. They are all fine soldiers & a credit to our Empire. (*These Indian soldiers had probably already taken part in the Battle of Neuve Chapelle 10 – 13 March 1915. After this battle 1685 Rifleman Gabar Singh Negi of the 2nd Battalion, 39th Garhwal Rifles was posthumously awarded a Victoria Cross. London Gazette, 28 April 1915: "During our attack on the German position he was one of a bayonet party with bombs who entered their main trench, and was the first man to go* round each traverse, driving back the enemy until they were eventually *forced to surrender. He was killed during this engagement. Rifleman Gabar Singh Negi's name is recorded on the Neuve Chapelle Memorial as Gobar Sing Negi.*) At 6 p.m. of this day we all embarked on board, after watching the guns being put aboard (a very interesting affair) on the transport steamer, S.S. Fameras, & at 6.45 p.m. left the docks for somewhere abroad. (*Even though the British Army had started to be motorised at the turn of the century, at this time it still relied heavily on a lot of horse power when going to war.*) The first half of the voyage was most beautiful but in the early hours of the morning, the sea became very rough indeed. There was about 250 horses on board. We went below and turned in for the night about 9 p.m. but all got very little sleep. Some were sea-sick but that did not occur to me. While out at sea I bought a ¼ lb tin of Capstan Navy Cut tobacco for 9d (*In today's money this would have cost £3.90p*). Two torpedo-boat destroyers escorted us across, but when Boulogne was sighted about 6 a.m. they turned about & were soon out of sight in the direction of England.

27th From 6 p.m. to about 10 a.m. we laid off the entrance to the harbour & waited for the high tide when we entered the dock. The guns were then landed. At 2p.m. we left the docks & proceeded by motor lorry to the rest camp outside the town. Directly on arrival 2 tents were allotted to the A.S.C. & we settled down for the night. My first experience of being under canvass. (*This may well have been the Camp near Etaples where soldiers of the British Army famously mutinied in 1917, the catalyst for the trouble was the way new arrivals were unjustly and brutally persecuted by the training staff in the Bullring Training area. The Permanent Staff were identified by the yellow bands around their peaked caps, and the maltreated soldiers who endured the training staff's dreadful conduct at the camp, often commented about the fact that the colour yellow was a sign of cowardice.*)

28th Here we awaited the arrival of the lorries from Avonmouth which arrived during the night of the 28th. In the morning we had a kit inspection & were afterwards served out with field bandages & emergency rations also 20 rounds of ammunition. (*Emergency/ Iron Rations consisted of a tin of preserved meat, cheese, biscuits, tea, sugar and salt. These items could only be opened in the event of being isolated from your unit for over 48 hours and when permission was granted by an Officer.*) The weather was bitterly cold here a wind blowing the whole of the time. We were stationed on the side of a hill above the town & the white cliffs of Dover could be distinctly seen. In the camp was a YMCA (**Young Men's Christian Association**) tent; which was very acceptable. Every night a short service was held which was generally well attended.

29th Packed our kit, & joined the lorries, which had been got off board in the early morning, about 10 a.m. & proceeded with the battery to (somewhere in the direction of the firing line). I might say here that the cars were all loaded before leaving Avonmouth as follows. 5 had 10 rounds of ammunition each & the other 4 had the stores. It turned out very hot in the morning & travelling, was a very dusty journey all the day. Arriving at Dervres (**probably Desvres**) we stopped for dinner & about 6 p.m. we arrived at Sen-lec-ques (**probably Senlecques**) where we put up for the night.

Here we were billeted in farmyards etc, & here I spent my 1ˢᵗ night in a barn amongst the straw, & none too acceptable either, for great rats were running all over in the dark. It caused much amusement though. (**The same billets were occupied by 13ᵗʰ Siege Battery about one month earlier and even at that time the place was condemned as accommodation, some of the straw palliasse's (mattresses) were burnt as a consequence. Two days later a Staff Officer arrived from General Headquarters to enquire about the damage done to his mattresses. Although condemned, the accommodation continued to be used as billets by the Rank & File soldiers of following units, but Officers were accommodated in the local Chateau. This information was taken from 13ᵗʰ Siege Battery's official War Diary dated 28th – 30th May 1915.**)

30th Continued our journey about 8 a.m. our next stop was at Auvevirquin (**possibly Ouve-Wirquin**) & then proceeded to Wavram (**probably Wavrans-sur-l'Aa**) for the night. Here I met with 2 young men from Driffield. For the night I slept on the shells in the lorry & found it very cold indeed. (**When closed up some of these convoys were at least 650 yards long and they often had to be re-routed because the French bridges just weren't robust enough to take the weight of the heavy-duty lorry's, howitzers, and ammunition cargo.**)

31st Continued journey about 10.30 a.m. & arrived at St Omer (General French's Headquarters) about noon. The caterpillars, guns & lorries were all stationed under cover of a plantation at St Martin's where we halted while the following morning. In the evening we were each paid 5 Francs (4/2d in English coin) (*Worth just under £50 in today's monetary comparison*) by 2nd Lieu (*Lieutenant*) Davidson. Our 1st pay this being on active service. It is a very nice country about here & St Omer is a fine old town & worth seeing. For the night we slept in a big building & had plenty of straw & this was a great benefit for we had a very good nights rest. (*Caterpillars were a tracked type vehicle that became Winston Churchill's inspiration for the 'Little Willie' tank, these impressive vehicles were used by the ASC to haul Heavy Artillery guns and trains of stores over French roads and ground that a lorry simply couldn't cope with. By 1918 over 10,000 had been used in a variety of roles. FWD (USA), Hornsby (UK) and Holts (USA) had supplied the British Army with a variety of designs and many had been imported from the United States and Canada. The 13 ton 'Little Caterpillar' could reach a speed of 15 mph and traversed even the worst of the Western Front locale's whilst easily pulling an 8 ton trailer.*

1st June 1915

Left St. Omer at 10 a.m. Broke the journey at Aire (*Aire-sur-la-Lys*), where we halted for dinner. Here I was watching a motor convoy pass & I happened to see Earnie (*Ernie*) pass. I caught him up but unfortunately I could not get many words with him. We were served out here with tobacco & cigarettes etc. About 2 p.m. we left the town & arrived at St. Hilliare (*probably Saint-Hilaire-Cottes*) where we halted for the night. The C.O. of 282 Company met us here & as we were very heavily loaded he sent us along two Daimlers to ease our lorries a little. For the night we slept in a barn in the hay-loft & the following morning the tenant gave us all coffee which was greatly appreciated.

2nd Left St. Hilliare at 8 a.m. & went along to Bethune where we stayed along the canal side while 7 p.m. Here we saw the first French observation balloon which created much interest. During the morning the town, which is a fairly large town, was shelled by the German guns about 11 a.m. About 7 p.m. the whole battery proceeded from here & took up there (*their*) position behind the firing line, at a village called Gore a few kilometres to the left of La Bassee. The lorries where emptied of all stores & all ammunition was left at the battery.

This was the first time we had been in the firing zone and shells where flying about all the time. An armoured train, near to here, was doing much firing. Leaving the battery, the lorries proceeded to Vendin, where we drew up by the roadside & after the guard had been mounted all turned in.

3rd Paraded before the C.O. of 282 Comp. & he informed us we were attached to his company for the duration of the war. This company is the 15th Brigade Ammunition Column & supplies shells etc to the 13th & the 19th Siege Batteries. He gave us orders regarding the lorries & informed us we were expected to keep them spotlessly clean. Afterwards we commenced the work, which has been so very tiring to us ever since, infact (**in fact**) it is a very monotonous procedure. Near to this place is a coal-pit. Moved from here to Vendin, a small village on the left of Bethune.

4th It is a very dirty village & like all French villages abounds with estaminets, or public houses. Many troops come round this vicinity from the trenches for a few days rest.

5th On this date our guns fired 15 rounds at La Bassee. During the morning cars were attended to.

6th Proceeded with lorry to Vendin to 282 Company where the workshops of company were & the lorry was thoroughly inspected by the fitters. In the evening returned to Essars.

7th Thoroughly cleaned lorry & in the afternoon went up to the battery & bought the mails back to Essars. Then took 3 drums of oil to Gore to the caterpillars. On this day I had my first bath if you could call it one. Having no bathroom, I had to revert to a bucket of water, which I used to the best advantage in the lorry. (**Having a stripped wash has been a routine that most**

soldiers, from every army throughout time, has had to endure whilst deployed into the field.)

8th Again thoroughly cleaned lorry. In the afternoon a very heavy thunderstorm took place & I never saw larger hailstones in my life. The village was flooded & we turned out & dug gullies to clear it all away. It did much good seeing the place was so dirty. This was our 1st wet day in France.

9th Met a Canadian soldier who comes from Walkington near Beverley & he informed me his 2 sisters have a public house in that village which I know quite well. Our company went to the La Bassee canal for a swim. There was much heavy gunfire in the evening & aeroplanes where very active indeed.

10th Usual routine of work. Had a German dumb dumb cartridge given me by a Canadian soldier whom I met. (*The original idea of the Dum Dum bullet occurred in a British Arsenal near Calcutta in 1890, the Hollowed-Point, or Flattened Head bullets, caused dreadful wounds on Britain's enemy's which led to the Hague Convention banning their use in International Warfare in 1899. Soldiers in the trenches didn't always abide by these laws.*) A very nice chap he was too. Being hard up for tobacco he gave me a ¼ tin which I was very pleased to receive. (*Canadian soldiers received a much higher rate of pay than their British comrades and could afford to be generous.*) Received my 1st letter from home. In the evening watched the Germans shelling our aeroplanes.

11th J. Brydon's lorry & our lorry proceeded to St Vennant (*probably Saint - Venant*) for ammunition in charge of Serg (*Sergeant*) Elliott. Here we were ordered to stay while further orders with 282 Company, who had removed from Vendin to the above village. St. Vennant is only a small town and a large amount of ammunition is brought up by rail from the base.

12th Here cars were thoroughly cleaned again seeing we were attached to Headquarters. Had another washing of clothes in the afternoon. I might say here this is one of our worse engagement which we always shirk.

13th Received a box of cakes etc from home. All the day a very heavy bombardment took place along the whole front. I shall ever remember this for in the distance it sounded as though it was thundering & it was one continual peal. Served out with tobacco & cigarettes also field service cards & a green envelope. This is done every Sunday afternoon. (*A journalist wrote in 'The War Illustrated' magazine that it was essential for everyone to correspond with soldiers at the front, "Letters from home are as essential in their way to a soldier in the field as food and supplies; for just as food is needed to keep him in fighting trim, so is news of relatives and friends to keep him in good spirits and fighting mood". All mail was censored by unit officers to make sure each letter didn't contain sensitive information about what was happening where the soldiers were fighting. In 1915, to ease the increasing work load of the sensors, a special Green Envelope (Army Form W3078) was issued for the soldiers to write home, the troops had to sign a certificate on the reverse of the envelope which stated, "I certify on my honor that the contents of this envelope refer to nothing but private and family matters". These 'Honor Envelopes' turned out to be very popular with soldiers because they knew their letters wouldn't be read by the sensors. Unsurprisingly, not every soldier was that honorable though.*)

14th Left Headquarters & proceeded to St. Vennant station & there took our 2nd load of ammunition (30 rounds) to Essars. Heard that our battery was doing very good work. (*The Thornycroft and Peerless vehicles could carry an average of thirty rounds of artillery ammunition in one load.*)

15th Thoroughly cleaned cars & prepared for our next journey. During the evening the Germans shelled our front very heavy & aeroplanes were very active. During the evening a French aeroplane was hit rather severely & in returning came down very sudden. On guard for the 1st time in France which was mounted at 7.p.m. & dismissed at 7 a.m. This was my 1st time on guard with rifle loaded (5 rounds).

16th Proceeded to St. Omer with ammunition where we joined the left half of our battery. In the afternoon the garrison men played the A.S.C. at cricket winning (96 runs to 35).

17th Cleaned cars as usual. In the afternoon had a game of rounders on the St. Omer recreation ground. At 6 p.m. the left half lorries took over our ammunition & we proceeded to Headquarters at St. Vennant with Corporal Norman in charge & arrived at 8.30 p.m.

18th Cleaned cars once more. During the day Bethune was shelled rather heavily resulting in several casualties but little damage to property. In the afternoon was a bathing parade.

19th Received my 1st Hull Times at the front & since then I have received it every week, much to my pleasure. Did 2nd guard. R Davies being in hospital I took his place. Helped to prepare a boxing ring in the field for the forthcoming event.

20th Our 2nd pay day on active service, each receiving 40 francs. Aeroplanes very active & were shelled in several instances from the German lines. It is very interesting to watch this very modern means of warfare. Bathing parade as usual.

21st Instead of the 6.15 a.m. march the Serg-major (*Sergeant- Major*) put us through a physical drill. At 9.30 a.m. Lieu (*Lieutenant*) Michael gave us a severe rifle drill for about 45 minutes then we proceeded with our usual work.

22nd Rifle drill again at 9.30. This was a terribly hot day & in the afternoon a thunderstorm crossed over. The Germans sent over two Jack Johnson's which fell about 2 miles off St. Vennant but doing no damage. (*A Jack Johnson was a German shell which exploded and emitted lots of black smoke, it was named after the first black American World Heavyweight boxing champion, Jack (John Arthur) Johnson (Born 1878 – died 1946)*).

23rd Parades & drill as usual. In the afternoon had the opportunity of having a bath, this was the 2nd on active service. In the evening took a walk through several trenches on the side of the canal bank.

24th Handed in rifle & took over a Canadian Ross rifle. These rifles have done good service in the firing line, but in quick-firing they get very hot, so the authorities took the A.S.C's rifles which were in good condition over & we have to take over the inferior rifle.

No. of my rifle is 1044 Pg. (*At this stage of the war there was a shortage of all sorts of equipment and in particular, rifles. The 'Behind the Lines' troops had to surrender their superior .303 Lee Enfield rifles to the Infantrymen fighting in the front-line trenches, the logistic troops were then issued with the inferior Canadian .303 Ross Rifle. Although the Ross was a very accurate weapon its firing mechanism was prone to jamming and it also had a slower rate of fire. Many Canadian troops replaced their Ross rifles with Lee-Enfield's taken from British casualties. By 1916 the shortage of rifles had been overcome and Field Marshal Haig ordered that all Canadian units should exchange their Ross Rifles with the superior British Lee Enfield.*)

25th Parades & drill etc. In the afternoon Lieu (*Lieutenant*) Michael inspected cars. Bathing parade at 2.00 p.m. In the evening took a stroll into St. Vennant.

26th Usual routine of work & drill. In the afternoon finished off the boxing ring for the match. A canteen was also put up close by for the use of the company. A piano was hired for the concert which followed the boxing contest. General's French & Joffre passed to-day. (*General Joffre was promoted to Chief of French General Staff in 1911 and after the Battle of Marne in 1914 he was declared 'The Saviour of France'. In 1915 he made a series of blunders in the hurriedly planned attacks against the German lines in Artois and Champagne. He was a very popular General with the French nation and so when dismissed from his duties in 1916, he was given the flattering and courteous appointment of 'The Marshal of France'.*)

27th Cars were cleaned in the morning. At 5 p.m. the contest took place. The most important event was a 10, 2 min round contest (Welter-weight) between Pte. J. Thompson (Bermonsey Cyclone) 1st D. S. C & Pte J. Donnatti (ex-amatuer-champion lightweight of Scotland,) of 282 Company the latter being declared the winner, Thompson retiring in the 3rd round. Other interesting contests took place & on the whole the proceeding were a great success. In the evening a good concert finished off the programme. (*Johnny Thompson was a professional fighter who had had ten professional fights between the years of 1907 – 1913. It remains unclear as to what the 1st D.S.C. means. The other fighter might possibly have been Bob Donati from Edinburgh, another professional fighter who had eighteen professional fights between 1913 and 1923.*)

28th Usual work. Heavy firing along the front. A quantity of comforts were received by our company from the Commercial Motor Comforts Fund & distributed amongst us. All drew lots & I drew for a pair of socks, but being much for large I gave them away. (*Many manufacturers in the UK organised soldier comforts like articles of clothing, sweets, tobacco, etc, and sent them out to the soldiers serving in France and Belgium. The comforts were supposedly for the benefit of our soldiers moral whilst at war, but in reality it didn't do the manufacturers' any harm in advertising their wares.*)

29th Did my 3rd Guard. The Observation Balloon near Bethune was shelled by the Germans & was slightly damaged, but had to be hauled down for repair.

30th The whole company packed up & removed from St. Vennant to Vendin. A very wet day indeed. All lorries were lined up by the side of the road. This was a busy day for us, as the cook-houses & the canteen, also the N.C.O tent had to be built.

1st July 1915

Cars were thoroughly cleaned, & the column was made as tidy as possible. Here the road is well shaded with large trees on both sides, which is the general practice of the French roads & this gives the lorries good cover from the enemies' aircraft. Near here is a small coal-pit called the Vendin Mine & we are about 2 kilometers (**kilometres**) from Bethune.

2nd Usual work in morning. Rifle drill in the afternoon. Here the lorries of the left half joined the company. In the evening 335 Company had a grand concert. This company is stationed in the coal-pit yard. Here I met the two brothers Robinson late of Hammonds & they are attached to the above company. The concert was a great success.

3rd Cars thoroughly cleaned. At 5 p.m. I was inoculated. This was my 2nd time. I was very ill on this occasion, but my arm was not at all painful. Given 48 hours sick leave.

4th Being on sick leave & not allowed to leave the column I could not attend Church Parade, which was the 1st opportunity our company had had of doing so in France. Several shells fell in Bethune on this date. A very hot day and greatly troubled with flies.

5th Drill order 11 a.m. Bad news heard of the loss of 3 British guns and 30 men. (**The Official War Diary states that the one Battery suffered damage and two guns were put out of action.**)

6th The Germans again shelled the Observation Balloon at Bethune. Leave starts for 282 Company.

7th Pte. Mick disappeared. The 2nd gun position of the left half of our battery was heavily shelled. A terrific wind storm. (**This gale is also logged into 13th Siege Battery's War Diary.**)

8th After the 8.30 a.m. parade we were told off to prepare for the passing of Lord Kitchener, but the Secretary of State for war did not pass our column.

(Field Marshal Lord Kitchener was the iconic face with the pointing finger on the recruiting posters of the First World War, the poster stated, "Britons. (Lord Kitchener) wants you. Join your country's army now. God save the King).

9th Our guns fired 60 rounds on this date. Rifle parade at 2.30 p.m. & went on a route march.

10th Usual work of the day. A very hot day too.

11th Unconditional surrender of the Germans in S.W Africa. 40 Motor Buses passed with troops for the front. A Church Parade at 2.30 p.m. *(The Treaty of Khorab entailed all German Forces surrendering to General Louis Botha on 9th July 1915, this in effect ended any German rule in South West Africa.)*

12th A letter from Sir Douglas Haig was received at company headquarters to the effect that Lord Kitchener on his recent visit to the troops at the front was satisfied with the appearance & work of the men.

13th Rifle drill. 38 Motor Buses full of troops passed. 2 large guns passed through. 1st Batt Kings' Royal Rifles went back to the trenches after a short rest. *(This unit move is mentioned in 13th Siege Battery's War Diary but is annotated as New Army.)*

14th Usual work. Parcel of cakes etc received from home.

15th Rifle drill in the morning. Lt. *(Lieutenant)* Stewart was rather severe in his instructions at drill. Leave is stopped for the column.

16th Rifle drill. Violent bombardment of aircraft. The Observation Balloon shelled. The Worcesters *(Worcester Infantry Regiment)* passed through on their way to the trenches. A French armoured car also passed. Heavy bombardment all the night.

17th Usual work.

18th 2 shells dropped in Bethune. Major Moberly passed the column in his car. Lots of wounded went through. Cricket match between the 7th Siege Battery & our company. They were defeated by 99 runs to 67.

19th Bethune shelled. Harvesting operations were in full swing.

20th Prince of Wales passed at 11 a.m. & asks "Why are these lorries not used?" A French funeral passed the column the 1st I had seen in France. Several loads of furniture went through. A good concert by 335 Company was held in the coal-pit.

21st Aeroplanes very active in the evening. Our 3rd pay day in France, receiving the usual 40 francs. Shells fell in Bethune again.

22nd The Germans again shelled Bethune, Lehay & Pte Ford had a narrow escape. 2 men talking to them were hit by fragments of a shell & injured.

23rd Raining all day. 2 lorries proceeded from the column to Bethune to clear up the mess. 2 coldstream (**Coldstream**) guards (**Guards**) killed in Bethune by a shell.

24th Cricket match & usual work.

25th Went to St, Vennant for 30 rounds of ammunition. Cricket match in the afternoon

26th Usual parades & work.

27th Took the 2nd load of ammunition to the guns. Left the column at 8 p.m. & arrived back at 11 p.m. A beautiful moonlight night & all was quite at the front, except a little rifle fire.

28th Thoroughly cleaned lorry. G.W. Sydenham left the left half & came to our lorry, as 3rd driver.

29th Aeroplanes very active & some heavily shelled.

30th Rifle drill in the afternoon. Prince of Wales passed. Piano came to the canteen & was greatly appreciated by all. J. Bohler's lorry went for new tires (Thornycroft).

31st Cricket match by A.S.C. & 5th Liverpools'. First court martial witnessed in the army. A private of the 5th Liverpools' was sentenced to death by a court martial, but the sentence was repealed to one of 6 months hard labour. (*The soldier in question is mentioned in 13th Siege Battery's war diary as Corporal Britton who had been Absent Without Leave, he must have been from another unit otherwise he would have been referred to in the diary's as a Bombardier. This was by no means the first British Army Courts Martial of the Great War, this honour went to Private Thomas Highgate of the Royal West Kent Regiment who was found hiding in a barn after the Battle of Mons late in August 1914. The ill-fated 17 year old was reputedly undefended at his Courts Martial and was more than likely suffering from the, as yet undiagnosed, Shell shock which is now called Post-Traumatic Stress Disorder. On the insistence of his own Officers, Private Thomas Highgate was swiftly executed in front of soldiers from the Dorset and Cheshire Regiments shortly after his hasty trial had been completed.)*

1st August 1915

Bethune shelled again. The usual work for day & concert in the evening at the canteen.

2nd Heard bad news from Russia. Received a box of sweets etc from my brother. (*The bad news from Russia may have been that the Russian army were continuously being beaten by the German and Austrian Armies and were consequently being pushed out of Poland*).

3rd 40 men of the company proceeded by motor lorries to Bethune to have a shower-bath, which was a real treat. (*Showers and baths were only taken when a unit had retired to the rear lines, these temporary tented facilities were built by the Royal Engineers with the help of the Army Service Corps and the Sanitary Section of the Royal Army Medical Corps. The RAMC handed over its part of this role in 1917. In those days most civilians only took a bath or shower once a week at the most anyway. If there weren't any facilities available for a resting Infantry unit then the soldiers would take a 'Whores Bath', this incorporated washing themselves in their helmet after filling it with water.*) Took a walk in the evening & just for curiosity we looked into an estaminet where a crowd of soldiers were gambling. (*Gambling was, and still is, an illegal pastime for soldiers both in and out of barracks.*)

4th In the afternoon went to Chocques with our cricket team to play the R.A.M.C, the result being a draw, 66 runs each after which the boys entertained us to tea.

5th Cricket match during the afternoon. Received a parcel from home. A rather heavy bombardment & aeroplanes very busy.

6th Bethune shelled again. Cricket match again. Received my breeches. Took a very pleasant walk in the evening to the aerodrome close by.

7th Heard of the fall of Warsaw. (*See 2nd August*) Cricket match in afternoon. Fetched away to proceed with lorry for ammunition from St. Vennant. Returned with 30 rounds. Did guard, my 4th time out here.

8th Aeroplanes very active indeed. The usual parades & work as usual. Noticed the Germans had 5 observation balloons up, observing our lines.

9th Rifle drill in the afternoon. Several motor ambulances passed the column with wounded. Bethune shelled, but little damage done.

10th Paraded at 6.15 a.m. & reported sick. Went at 8.30 a.m. to Chocques to the medical officer & was attended to, afterwards returning to the column by one of the motor ambulances. This was my first ride in a vehicle as that, & I formed a very good opinion of the cars. Concert in the evening at Chocques, my friend George singing 2 songs.

11th The store lorry left the column & proceeded to Cambrin to do some work for the Royal Engineers. Watched our aeroplanes being shelled by the Germans in the evening.

12th The usual parades & work of the day. Nothing doing to speak of, all being quite, as though there was no war going on.

13th Giving an hours rifle drill in the afternoon by Serg. (*Sergeant*) Elliott. Had a stroll in the evening. A very hot day.

MODEL T FORD AMBULANCE

14th The ambulances were again busy also our airmen were very active. A German Taube flew over our lines & crossed over above our column. (*In the diary Frank refers to every aircraft he spots as a Taube, but in-actual fact there must have been an assortment of German aircraft. The Taube (German word for Dove) was initially built in the early 1900's and served in the German Army as a spotter plane in 1914. It was very underpowered and soon became obsolete as aircraft design and development accelerated in the early stages of World War One. The Taube is famous for carrying out the very first bombing raid on Paris in 1914.*)

15th A Church Parade in the morning a very heavy shower just after we arrived back. Took a walk in the evening & visited a cemetery where several officers & men of a London regiment were buried. (*Chocques Commonwealth War Graves Cemetery.*)

16th Parades & cleaning of cars as usual. Nothing to be seen of any importance, but the aeroplanes.

17th A battalion of Kitchener's Army (the 8th Berkshire's) passed on their way to the front & it was a very fine sight. All the men were in the best of spirits & it did one good to see them.

18th Parades & usual work. Dual in the air by 2 aeroplanes & the British aircraft heavily fired at.

19th The whole of the Guards Brigade returned from the front & went back to St. Omer to be formed into a division. Aeroplane of the Germans dropped bombs in Bethune & flew right over our column at a great altitude.

20th Parades & usual work. A very wet day. 4th pay day receiving 40 francs.

21st Nothing of any importance occurred.

22nd Parades as usual. Rifle drill by 2nd Lieu. (*Lieutenant*) Young in the afternoon.

23rd Heavy bombardment by the British. Met a Hull man who was in the Guards (Coldstream).

24th Store lorry out all day carting store etc for the Royal Engineers. General French passed the column. Got writing paper from M.C.F. (*Motor Comfort Funds - see 28th June 1915.*)

25th Met Corporal Neal of the Hertfordshire Regiment who were billeting down in the village of Vendin. He is a friend of G.W.S. & we had an enjoyable time together. Heard of British success in the Baltic. The Germans losing several ships. (*This entry in the diary is probably referring to the Royal Navy's* *success at sinking several German ships that were transporting Iron Ore from Sweden to Germany.*)

26th Several privates made a commotion regarding their badges & were paraded before the W.O. & dismissed luckily for them, because they would have been punished if they had to go before the captain. Did my 5th Guard.

27th The guns were removed from Gore to Sally-le-Bore (*possibly Sailly-Labourse*). This is on the extreme right of the British lines, next to the French.

28th The guns were put in position at the above place. Heard that there were about 90 guns to the mile at that place.

29th 4 (*four*) 8" howitzers of the 23 Siege Battery passed. These guns went into the position vacated by our guns. The 1st Royal Berk's, 1st King's Royal, rifles & the 1st South Staffords passed on their way to the front. Great boxing match held at Lilliars (*Lillers*).

30th 5 batteries of 18 pounder's went up to the front, all new out from England.

31st Nothing to report.

1st September 1915

The whole column moved off from the Bethune road & took up a position at Lepugnoy (*Lapugnoy*). A rail-head at the above place.

2nd A very wet day & the whole surrounding place was very dirty. Issued with smoke helmets. (*These smoke helmets were a simple khaki material bag that had been soaked in chemicals to protect soldiers from chlorine gas, the manufacturers also added an oblong celluloid window for visibility. The bag was simply tucked into the soldiers' uniform to provide protection from any* *poisonous-gases, and as he breathed, air was forced through the material so he could breathe a more purified atmosphere. This was the fore-runner to the Ph Helmet which protected against later Phosgene Agents, the so called smoke helmets/hoods and Hypo Helmets were the very first versions of what eventually became the 'Gas Mask'.)*

3rd Heard bad news from the battery. Divine & Bradley, 2 gunners, were accidentally killed by a dug out falling in on Sept 1st.

4th Met with the L.R.B. (*London Rifle Brigade*) boys & had a jolly time together.

5th Captain Drysdal (*Possibly Drysdale*) paraded us & we were given instructions to keep all things quiet & not to speak to anyone regarding the war. Church Parade.

6th 3 lorries of the 23rd Siege Battery blown up by the Germans. A very hot day. Busy laying stone on the road side to keep the lorries from bogging.

7th Nothing of any interest to note.

8th Usual work of cleaning lorries.

9th Took a walk round the Lapugnoy & visited a cheateua (*chateau*). Which had been burnt down. Went to the guns that night with 30 rds (*rounds*) of ammunition under the charge of Serg. (*Sergeant*) Fisher & Corp. (*Corporal*) Fowles.

10th Moved to Marles-le-Mines. A decent sized town but as usual very dirty, like all the French towns.

11th Had to parade in the morning with smoke helmets & respirator. Shaw took the men from our battery to St. Vernnant (*Saint Venant*), who had volunteered for French mortar work. A great Russian victory under the Czars command reported. A very heavy bombardment on the whole front.

12th Church Parade in the morning. Had a pleasant walk in the evening. A battery of the R.F.A. (London) stationed nearby.

13th Commenced with rifle drill every morning at 9.30 a.m. while 11.a.m. This is a new order, as it is said by the officers the company were getting very slack in this drill.

14th Usual parades & work, a very hot day indeed. Nothing of any interest to note.

15th This day passed the same as preceding day.

16th Rifle drill as usual. The whole company are always on parades for the rifle drill now. Before each section was drilled by its own sergent (*sergeant*).

17th Noticed the 15th A.S.C. column passing & happened to see two Hull drivers on it, who I knew quite well. Shower bath Bethune.

18th Issued with a pair of new boots. Usual parades, drill, & work etc for the day. Called up at 11.30 p.m. along with 5 other lorries & proceeded to Lepugnoy to draw ammunition 30 rounds each lorry. The rail-head very busy indeed. Arrived back at 1.30 p.m. & turned in once more.

19th A fleet of aeroplanes set off from the aerodrome near Auchel, 10 in number & proceeded in the direction of the firing line, as if carrying out a great raid. This was about the 1st time I had seen such a number turning out at once & it was a great site. A Church Parade in the morning. This was the 1st time one of our officers accompanied us.

20th Usual work but no rifle drill. The same thing occurred again in (paid 50 francs) the evening at 5.30 p.m. About 12 aeroplanes again went off on an air raid. They were the large Farman battle aeroplane. (*These were likely to be the Farman MF 11 Shorthorn that was used by both the French Airforce and the Royal Flying Corps. It was a French designed pusher aircraft that was crewed by a pilot and an Observer/Gunner who was armed with 1 x .30 inch machinegun and 18 x 16lb bombs. By 1916 the Farman MF 11 was relegated to training duties because its top speed of 66 mph made it easy prey for the much faster German fighters.*) The serg-major (*Sergeant Major*) went through the column practically, about 9 p.m. & caught several men smoking in ammunition lorries. This is a company order & strictly prohibited. Another shower bath.

21st The privates & N.C.O's so caught were paraded before the captain in the morning. The privates <u>awarded</u> 3 days 2nd field punishment & the N.C.O's were reprimanded. Heavy bombardment on the whole front. (*1st and 2nd Field Punishment were pretty much the same thing and involved a punished soldier being shackled in handcuffs, fetters, or in some cases both. The punishment was carried out for two hours every day but never more than three out of any four consecutive days. The only difference between the two punishments was that those on 1st Field Punishment were secured to a fixed object like a post.*)

22nd Usual work. The captain inspected the whole company & gave orders for new clothes to those who required them. A very heavy bombardment. Proceeded to the guns along with 5 other lorries at 5 p.m. with ammunition. This was my 2nd time at the guns in their new position. It is only about 2,000 yards from the trenches & the buildings are in a dreadful state, caused by shell fire of the enemy.

23rd Arrived back at 12.30 p.m. Proceeded for shell, 30 rounds, from Lepugnoy rail-head. Got the lorry ready for the next journey to the battery. 12 lorries left the column at 4.45 p.m & proceeded to the guns. On the way a heavy thunderstorm passed over. A heavy bombardment all along the front & the French 75's were to be heard firing very frequently. The guns fired 10 rounds about 11 p.m. This was the 1st time they had fired after dark, but having a special target they risked the conciquences (*consequences*). Arrived back at 4.30 a.m. the following morning.

24th Got up at 8 a.m. & got lorry ready for next journey. This made us very busy, working all day & greater part of the night, so the sergent (*sergeant*) told us to get as much sleep as possible. Went to the rail-head for ammunition drawing 30 rounds as usual about 6 p.m. The Battalion of York & Lancaster's passed the column on their way to the front. Left for the guns with the shells at 8 p.m. Whole battalion's and batteries of troops newly out from England were on their way to the front, it was a very difficult & a very trying job driving. Went by a new road to the battery through the French lines. There is a cemetery near the battery & the 2 gunners who were accidentally killed are buried their (*there*), so I went & had a glance at their graves. Such a beautiful cemetery & I shall ever remember that sight. Arrived back at 4.30 a.m. the next morning.

25th Heard good news of a general advance. An awfully wet day. The left half guns of the battery removed from the present position & took up a position a few kilometres to the left of the right half on Quality St, as this road is called. Heard that 2 men of this half of the battery had gone on duty drunk & were put under arrest to await court martial, the Major remarking that he would not have such men in the battery. 6 prisoners were taken by the R.G.A. being caught in a dug-out. Many Germans found in the dug-outs & taken prisoners by our troops. A large amount of cavalry passed through Marles, namely, 18th Hussars'; 11th, & 3rd Hussars, 16th, 9th, 21st Lancers; 5th Royal Irish Lancers; Kings' 1st Dragoon Guards & 2nd Dragoon Guards (Queens Boys) & 4th Royal Irish Dragoon Guards. The Guards Brigade, (Infantry) passed the town end on their way to the firing line. 1st full night in bed on 3 nights.

26th At 12.30 a.m. proceeded to Neux-le-Mines (***probably Noeux-les-Mines***) for ammunition drawing 33 rounds. 2 other lorries accompanied us, under the charge of Lieu (***Lieutenant***) Stewart. Saw a terrible lot of wounded this day & this was with the big attack which by this date has commenced in ernest (***earnest***). Arrived at the guns (left half) in Quality St about 7.30 p.m. & on the return journey brought to the field hospital, 5 wounded on stretchers, who had fallen during the day. I shall ever remember this sight & I got an idea of what this war is really like. Arrived home 1 a.m.

27th Cleaned the car & thoroughly over-hauled everything. Heard that all was going well at the front & that the British & French had taken 20,000 prisoners. Issued with a new cap & a pair of trousers.

28th The usual work of the day. The 1st Cavalry Division took up its Headquarters here. 2 lorries went to the guns with 60 rounds of ammunition. W. Redpath showed me a rifle captured from the Germans. (***This may have been one of three rifles that were used by the Germans in World War One, a 7 x 57mm Monragon rifle, a 7.92 x 57mm Gewehr 1888 rifle, or the 7.92 x 57mm Gewehr 98 rifle. In comparison, none of these rifles came close to the efficiency and effectiveness of the British Lee Enfield rifle.***) A very wet day & so wet at night that the 8.30 p.m. roll-call was abandonded (***abandoned***).

29th A very wet day again, heard that La Bassee was taken by us. The 11th Hussars & the 2nd Dragoon Guards, also battery of 13 pounders; (Royal Horse Artillery) passed, at full gallop. A German prisoner brought into the town by soldiers, who found him wandering on the road, when returning from the front.

30th The French made an advance in Champagne, taking 1 army corps, & making 23,000 prisoners. A 1,000 Germans said to have surrendered. Heard they had captured an important junction through which most of the German supplies for the Western Front had to come. Sorry to report that Goodwin (Pte) one of the left half caterpillar mechanic's had been severely wounded by a shell & succumbed to his injuries. No's 3 & 4 Section parade at 2'0clock with full kit for inspection. A very wet night & no roll-call.

1st October 1915

A very busy day. Called out at 4.30 p.m. to proceed to the right half guns, with the understanding that they were removing to a new position. The 9 lorries of the right half went & arrived at the guns at 7 p.m. We were not wanted, returning at 8 pm & getting back at 11. p.m. A very cold night. The left half guns came back from Quality St to their old position (near the right half guns). They were too near the firing line & could not fire for fear of the Germans finding their position.

2nd 25 British aeroplanes counted in the sky & all going in the direction of the firing line, most likely carrying out an extensive air-raid. A most imposing sight & the noise of the engines could be heard most distinctly in the distance. Heard that the French had taken over from the British several miles of trenches.

3rd Bethune shelled by the Germans with 17" shells. Heard that the 9.2 gun of the 13th Siege Battery which burst on the 25th September had been brought back to Bethune.

The Commercial Motor Comforts Fund sent a box of comforts to our company & were distributed amongst the men. Had an issue of rum for the 1st time after the roll-call at 8.30 p.m. as it was very cold. Green envelopes stopped being issued.

4th 3 Thornycroft lorries were brought from Aire to our company for the use of the 19th Siege Battery; as we are really short of lorries when busy. During the night of this date there was a violent bombardment. Russia issued a 24 hour's ultimatum to Bulgaria. G.W.S. applied for a commission. Filled in a paper as to when & for how long I joined the army.

5th A very wet day. No's 1 & 2 sections had a route march under the command of 2nd Lieu (*Lieutenant*) Stewart. In the evening there was a concert promoted by the W.O. of the company & the artistes were all men of the company. A very enjoyable evening & patronised by our officers.

6th No's 3 & 4 sections & Headquarters staff had a 4 miles route march under the command of 2nd Lieu (*Lieutenant*) Young. A whole division of R.F.A. (*Royal Field Artillery*) came into the town into rest-camp from the front after going through the recent engagement.

7th Usual work & parades etc. Nothing of interest to note. No's 1 & 2 sections had a route march. Heard that the Germans were shelling Masingarb (*Mazingarbe*) heavily.

8th Lieut (*Lieutenant*) Stewart & several men of the company had a game of hockey with the men of 256 company. Proceeded to Lepugnoy rail-head & loaded with ammunition at 4 p.m. At 7 p.m. 10 lorries went to the battery with shells. Pte Shaw, on 47 lorry, had engine trouble on the way, his oil not circulating. The Germans had shelled the vicinity of our battery during the day with gas shells & the men of the battery wore their respirators most of the day. Pte Annett on a store lorry, was slightly affected with the gas. The Germans hit a French armoured-train during the day badly damaged it, it being still burning when we were at the battery. The Germans attacked on the front & we could hear the rifle fire & it was pretty hot while it lasted. Arrived back at 4 p.m. The W.O. (*Warrant Officer*) & Serg (*Sergeant*) Elliott were in charge. A very dark night & roads very greasy.

9th Arose about 10 a.m. & prepared lorry for the next journey. A grand concert held in a hall in the town & was a great success & greatly enjoyed by the company. No roll-call.

10th A heavy bombardment on the whole front the whole day. A football match with 256 company in the afternoon. Heard of a great success by the French.

11th Usual work & parades. Gave in my respirator. Heard that the Germans had lost very heavy, about 8,000 dead, in the recent counter-attacks on the British & French & that of 70 prisoners captured at one time only one was above the age of 17.

12th Lieu (*Lieutenant*) Stewart was promoted 1st Lieutenant. No's 3 & 4 sections &Headquarters had rout march & rifle drill. Proceeded to Lepugnoy at 2 p.m. for shell & received 30 rounds. Was on guard for the 6th time & this time with rifle not loaded. Served out with a new smoke helmet. A meeting held in the canteen, to form a committee, to arrange for sports to take place through the winter. A very nice day & not at all cold. Lieu (*Lieutenant*) Quick returned to his unit.

13th Football match in the afternoon. 6 lorries with 30 rounds each of shell, proceeded to the battery leaving the column at 5.30 p.m. & arriving back at 11 p.m. record time. Our guns were in action when we arrived. Told that they were firing on La Bassee. In the distance could be seen Lens on fire, a very impressive sight, a town held by the Huns. A heavy bombardment on the whole front. Heard that our guns had been lent by our Government to the French, as the French hold that part of the line in front of our battery.

14th Football match again. A heavy bombardment again. Notice to the effect that following this date no 6.15 a.m. parade for the future. Serg. (*Sergeant*) Elliott promoted Serg-Major (*Sergeant-Major*) , & Serg-Major (*Sergeant-Major*) Cornwall reduced (own request) to Sergent (*Sergeant*)), & took over charge of No. 3 section.

15th A very nasty fog & the lorries were very rusty through it. A very unpleasant job to get it off as the issue of waste is stopped at present. J. Kynaston went home on special leave to see his wife & 2 kiddies who were very ill. An issue of rum. A French soldier, was buried at the cemetery here (Marles) & it was a very large funeral. The 1st Division came out of action, taking up headquarters here.

(Special leave was rarely granted and in most cases it was arranged because of the death, or serious illness of a close family member. Temporary 2nd Lieutenant Tom Adlam of the 7th Battalion Bedfordshire Regiment was informed his mother had died whilst serving on the Somme in 1916. The Adjutant told him, "By the time you get back home the funeral will be over old boy, she must be buried by now, you can't do any good at home so I advise you to stay here". Within days of having this conversation with his Adjutant, 2nd Lieutenant Tom Adlam was to win the Victoria Cross at Thiepval.)

16th 2 British submarines sunk 2 German ships in the Baltic. 5 lorries proceeded at 3.30 p.m. to the battery & No. 2 gun was removed at 6 p.m. to a new position near Masingarb, our lorry was not required & we all arrived back at 10 p.m. Given a half holiday by the C.O. & a football match took place in the afternoon. A battalion of French colonial troops passed through Marles & one formed a very good opinion of them, all were a happy lot. The London Batteries of field artillery went into action.

17th Thoroughly cleaned lorry & prepared for the next journey. Some of our lorries went to rail-head for ammunition. Holy Communion service held at 7.45 a.m. Church Parade at 6 p.m. Took a walk in the evening to Lepugnoy.

18th Rifle drill at 9.30 a.m. by 2 Lieu. (*Lieutenant*) Young. In the evening the Regimental Band of the 1st Division played to the officers outside their billet, from 7.30 p.m. to 10 p.m. Although it was a very cold night the men of our company listened very attentively to it, for it was a splendid band. The guard took into custody 2 artillery privates for being helplessly drunk in their lines. (*Depending on the mood of their Commanding Officer, these men could have been awarded up to 28 days Field Punishment, up to 28 days detention, or even worse, a loss of up to 28 day's pay. Extra Guard duties or a severe reprimand could also be added to the sentence.*)

19th Usual work in the morning, No's 1 & 2 sections had a route march. Hockey match in the afternoon with 256 Company, the latter winning. Several batteries of artillery of the 1st Division left this vicinity for new billets there being no room for them here. 2 lorries went to battery with shell. Headquarters, & No's 3 & 4 sections had a route march.

20th Paid 40 francs. Rugby football match. A grand concert in the cinema hall by 256 Company. A very good concert but did not go. Nothing of any interest occurred.

21st Usual work. The 1st Division Band played in the afternoon several selections in the town. 2 lorries proceeded to battery with shell. Subscribed 5 francs towards the sports committee. A very nice day. Aeroplanes very busy. In the evening took a walk into Auchel.

22nd A very shower of rain. Drill parade as usual. Made a petrol lighter of a German cartridge. (*These were commonly made by soldiers in the First World War and Frank in particular would have had access to all the engineering facilities available at 282 Company's Workshop.*) Football in afternoon (282 Company & the Caterpillar A.S.C. men) the 1st named winning 7 goals to 1. W. Redpath gave me a German rifle, captured at the Battle of Loos on September 26th.

23rd Mechanical inspection of lorries by section officers at 11 a.m. 2 lorries went to battery with shell (22nd) also 2 went up tonight. Football match at Vendin between our team & the 25th Brigade Ammunition Column. Result 3 – 3 goals. Paraded at 9.30 a.m. in drill order.

24th Headquarters & the 4 sections then had a route march to Auchel & back. The first time on a Sunday this was, that the whole company paraded in drill order. The band was to have led the way, but it was dismissed at the last moment, being too cold. Roman Catholics went to church at 9.30. Holy Communion at 8 a.m. & Church service at 6 p.m. A very wet day. Football match in the afternoon. 2 lorries took shell to battery.

25th Raining all day. No parades, but the role-call at 8.30 p.m. 3 lorries took shell to the battery. Heard that several of the R.G.A. men had returned to England to form a new battery. Our lorry took 30 rounds of ammunition to No. 2 gun at Fosse-three (*a fosse is a French term for a long, narrow trench or excavation, especially in a fortification*). Told that a shell had dropped a few yards from this gun in the afternoon, but no damage done. A very wet journey. Left the column at 3 p.m. & arrived at 6 p.m.

26th A fine day. Paraded at 9.30 a.m. in drill order, but dismissed. Commenced to clean lorry, which was covered in mud. Bethune heavily shelled by the Germans & much damage done. Could hear the shells dropping. 3 lorries took ammunition to the battery. Staff Serg. (*Staff Sergeant*) Gould gave a lecture on how to play Rugger football in the dinner hour. The sergents (*sergeants*) went into billet for the winter.

27th Commenced to parade in drill order at 8.30 a.m. as a standing order. Went for a route march. Proceeded to rail-head for ammunition. At 3 p.m. left the column & proceeded to Fosse-three via Chocques & Bethune to No. 2 gun. Very bad travelling. Arrived back at 7.p.m. Heavy firing by the guns along the front.

28th 2 lorries went to St. Vennant (Saint - Venant) for ammunition. 4 lorries took shell to battery. A very wet day & spent the day keeping dry & warm in lorry as best we could. Some officers entertained us in the evening in a small hall with a cinemato-graph & we greatly enjoyed it (*The cinemato-graph was a motion picture camera and projector that was invented in 1892*). The King passed through the town on his way to the front at 11.a.m.

29th Route march in drill order at 8.30 a.m. Proceeded to rail-head along with 3 other lorries to draw ammunition at 10 a.m. A very nice day. Heard that in a recent attack the French had inflicted enormous losses on the Germans. 4 lorries went to battery. (*This was an Anglo/French offensive in Artois and Loos*).

30th Usual march at 8.30 a.m. Football match at 2.30 p.m. against 26th Brg. Amm. Col. (*26th Brigade Ammunition Column*) Result (Draw). 3 lorries took shells to battery & we took 20 rounds to Fosse-three. Left column at 3 p.m & arrived back at 6.30 p.m. Heard of an accident to his Majesty (*The King was thrown from one of General Haig's horses and His Majesty had to be evacuated back to England on a stretcher*).

31st Parade at 8.30 a.m. Lieu (*Lieutenant*) Stewart headed the parade. Church Parades as last Sunday. Major Blackburn addressed us. 2 lorries went to battery with shell. Football match to have taken place at Aire but postponed. Very showery the weather.

1st November 1915 Very busy. Drew 30 rounds of ammunition from rail-head. Proceeded to battery along with 1 other lorry at 3 p.m. Arrived back 8.30 p.m. Teaming with rain the whole journey. The guns fired several rounds while we were there. Serg. (*Sergeant*) Fisher was given the opportunity to fire one of the guns. Compression tap broke off the front cylinder of our engine on the way home. Passed whole regiments of French troops on their way to the trenches. Issued with a new shirt & fur-coats were given to each man. (*During the winter season British soldiers were issued with a leather jerkin and greatcoat to keep warm, but because the weather in France sometimes dropped to minus 20 degrees, they were temporarily issued with animal fur jackets. Unfortunately, although these garments kept the soldiers very warm they were a breeding ground for even more body lice.*)

2nd The 2 store lorries were loaded with shells, because through the bad conditions of roads the Peerless performed the work much better than the Thornycroft. A very wet day. 9 men of the company were awarded pack-drill for different offences. (*Pack drill involved the offenders parading with their rifles whilst wearing their full kit and being marched up and down a parade ground for about an hour. Doesn't sound too bad, but whilst carrying 120lb of equipment you soon work up a sweat. Soldiers of the British Army came up with an expression to avoid being awarded these punishments, "No names, no pack drill". If all offenders remained silent and didn't bear witness to the offence, then no-one could be punished.*)

3rd Foot-ball match & given a half holiday in the afternoon. The visiting team won by 4 goals to 3. 2 lorries took ammunition to the guns. Was on guard for the 7th time. The workshop staff went into billets for the winter.

4th Parades as usual. Proceeded at 10 a.m. to battery with empty lorry, to carry stone to repair road to guns. On the way passed a French battery of 6" guns. They were taking up their position the same evening. A very fine lot of men they were. Took 2 load of stone to the road. Corp. (*Corporal*) Hay was in charge. Our guns were in action while we were there. Climbed to the top of fosse, & saw a hole where a German shell had dropped. Picked up several bits. A grand view of the country all round. 2 lorries took ammunition to the guns. Arrived back at 6 p.m. after a good days work and we were very glad. Aeroplanes were very active.

5th Proceeded to rail-head for 30 rounds of ammunition. Gave in to store our kakhi (*khaki*) great coats. Issued with 1 pair socks, 1 pair soles & gas goggles. 2 lorries went to guns with ammunition. Washed lorry down. During the night there was a heavy fog & sharp frost, the first frost of the winter. The W.O. (*Warrant Officer*) went home on leave.

6th Usual parades & work. 1 lorry went to battery with shell. Heard that Lord Kitchener passed through the town. Rugby foot-ball match in the afternoon & given a half holiday. Heard also that leave was to commence for the column. Commenced to parade at 7.30 a.m. for breakfast.

7th Church Parades as usual. Route march at 8.30 a.m. A fine day but very cold. Pte (*Private*) Vosper sent to battery to drive the Major's car. Nothing of an importance to note.

8th Parades as usual for the day. 2 lorries went to battery with shells. 1 lorry got ditched & a little further on the steering broke on the other car. Both left half lorries. Proceeded to Fosse 2, along with 1 other lorry with ammunition. This position had been heavily shelled just before we arrived but no damage done to the battery. Left column at 2.30 p.m & arrived back at 6 p.m. Pte (**Private**) Richardson sent to the battery to keep the motor-cycles in order. Foot-ball in the afternoon against the London Scottish, our team winning. The captain gave us orders on the 2 p.m. parade, & told us not to buy tinned fruit or meat in the town as there were several cases of foot and mouth disease in the vicinity.

9th The steering taken off our car & taken to the lorry which had broken down, to get it back to the column. Usual 8.30 a.m. route march. Washed the lorry down. G.W. Sydenham removed from our lorry to 43 lorry as second driver, in Pte (**Private**) Richardson's place. Lieu (**Lieutenant**) Young drew the names of the men to go on leave, on the 2 p.m. parade. 2 lorries proceeded to battery with ammunition.

10th Route march at 8.30 a.m. The fitters put our steering up again. 1 Lorry took ammunition to the battery. Got very wet on parade. A nasty wet day & nothing doing of any importance. Issued with bags for helmet. (***With the escalation of Gas War-fare, more and more chemical equipment was being issued to the soldiers on the Western Front. The bag meant each soldier would be able to carry his smoke or Ph helmet whilst working and have it close to hand without encumbering him.***)

11th All day raining. Nothing doing. 1 lorry went to battery with 30 rounds of ammunition. All kinds of tinned fruit, milk, etc also cigars, matches, & cigarettes & shaving requisites, were bought by the officers & placed in the canteen for the men of the company to buy.

12th Parades as usual, but dismissed on account of the rain. Proceeded to Lepugnoy for ammunition, drawing 30 rounds. 1 lorry took shells to the guns. Our guns very busy firing, also the French batteries in the vicinity. The Germans were sending several shells over & they were dropping very near our position. In the afternoon the company were given a half holiday as a football match had been arranged between our team & 256 company's team. It was a return match the result of last game being a draw. Highly enjoyed & the result was again a draw of 1 goal each. The men of our company took up mechanical horns, petrol cans & speaking horns, also a cornet or two from the band, & as much noise as possible was made, but for all the shouting etc we were unlucky in not winning.

13th So wet that there was no parade & very windy. Issued with a rubber cap cover. Cleaned lorry & prepared for next journey. Several lorries went to the battery as the 3 guns were removing from Bully Grenay. Left column at 3 p.m. & arrived back at 2 a.m. 1 gun was removed to Fosse 3 to the other stationed there & the other 2 went back to the old position at Gore. One gun in going over a bridge slipped to one side & dropped in the ditch. A very difficult task getting the guns out of the old positions & it took 3 caterpillars to move them.

14th Several lorries went to the position the guns had left to bring all the battery tools, etc, to the new positions, left at 2 p.m. & arrived back at 12 midnight. A very sharp frost during the night. Went to Auchel in the afternoon for a walk. Church Parades cancelled.

15th The usual parades. The 1st Division Headquarters left the town & went into action & the 47the Division came out of action & took up head-quarters in the 1st Division's place. Many troops passed through the town & the transports were very busy. The gun in the dyke at Gore was got out & placed in position.

16th Very cold day & awfully wet. On the 2 p.m. parade Lieu (*Lieutenant*) Stewart gave orders to the effect that if the underneath of the lorries were not kept cleaner, we should be severely punished. 3 lorries went to Gore with ammunition.

17th Cleaning lorries as usual. In the afternoon, foot-ball match with R.A.M.C. our team winning 4 goals to 1. A fine day & aeroplanes were very active. Nothing of any interest occurred. Practice hockey-match.

18th Parades as usual. At 11 a.m. Lieu (*Lieutenant*) Young inspected the tool kits of lorries of 19th Siege Battery. At 2 p.m. went to Gore to right half guns with ammunition. A very wet afternoon. All very quiet at the front. Told that the gun which had been in the dyke & as understood to be damaged, had during the day had 3 direct hits. Returned to the column at 6 p.m. Several batteries of artillery passed through the town.

19th A very busy day. Very cold & dirty. Foot-ball match against 1st Siege Battery at 2 p.m. Result 4 goals to1. A most violent bombardment along the front all the day.

20th Cleaning lorries all day. Our foot-ball team visited Choques in the afternoon & played the R.A.M.C. of the 12th M.A.C. (***Motor Ambulance Convoys – these were Army Service Corps units that were attached to a Casualty Clearing Station, each ASC ambulance was manned by one ASC driver and an RAMC attendant.***) A walk over our team winning 5 goals to nil. Was on guard for the 8th time. The joiners made sentry boxes for the guard to shelter in & the same were placed in position in the column.

21st Paid 50 francs. A church parade for the R C's (*Roman Catholics*) at 10 a.m. At 2 p.m. orders came, for the 6 ammunition lorries of the right-half battery were to proceed to Verdin & park up along the road, where we had been parked before & to stay there till further orders. After drawing rations & stores we left the column & arrived there about 4 p.m. All sorry to leave Marles-le Mines, for the people were very good to us. Heavy gun-fire all day.

22nd Had no parades, seeing we were away from head-quarters. Very busy all day. Building a cook house etc. We were in charge of Serg (*Sergeant*) Cornwall & Corp (*Corporal*) Hay. 16 men all told. There was again much heavy gunfire all the day. During the night a very sharp frost & very foggy. Heard that 8 A.S.C. (***Army Service Corps***) men had been killed at a certain rail-head by an 8" shell dropping & exploding. (***When collecting artillery ammunition at the rail-head the shells weren't loaded onto the lorry's with any sort of Mechanical Handling Equipment. The individual shells were man-handled***

onto the back of the trucks without any sort of packaging and they were simply stacked on the load area. On arrival at the guns they were basically rolled off the back of the lorry using a narrow plank of wood. This was very labour intensive and dangerous work carried out by both the Royal Artillery Gunners and Army Service Corps drivers.) No 50 lorry on the way to Marles collided with another car, & this broke one of the front springs of the lorry. 2 lorries went to battery to fetch away ammunition. The pins on the pump drive, on our lorry & 49 lorry broke. Lorry 51 had the same thing happen.

23rd No parades seeing the 6 lorries were away from the rest of the company. Dug a large hole in the bank on the side of the main road. 16 ft by 22 ft by 6 ft. This is a dug-out & we are to finish it so that we have somewhere to sit & suing (*I cannot understand what Frank means by suing but it is definitely what he's written.*) we can have a fire in, we are anticipating being very comfortable. Received a parcel from home. Thaw set in & made the ground very dirty. Several armoured cars passed the column.

24th Busy making the dug-out. On guard for the 9th time, for 4 hours (7 p.m. to 11 p.m. & then went off duty. Ambulances were very busy & many wounded passed the column. Several batteries of field artillery came out of action & passed here, coming back for a rest. <u>Mails lost</u>.

25th Went to Marles-le-Mines to our headquarters for stores etc for the 6 lorries stationed at Vendin. Several privates in the column were promoted lance-corporals. Corp (*Corporal*) Fearn promoted quarter-master sergeant. Went to battery in the evening with Pte (*Private*) Shaw on 46 lorry in place of R Crook who is ill. Took ammunition, leaving the column at 6 p.m. & arriving back at 8 p.m. Finished making the dug-out.

26th Proceeded to the rail-head for ammunition. During the night a very sharp frost. A heavy fall of snow about mid-day. Aeroplanes very busy & much heavy artillery-fire.

27th No's 46, 48, & 43 lorries left the column at 6 a.m. & took ammunition to the guns. A very sharp frost & most difficult starting the engines. Got back at 8 a.m. & directly after breakfast all 6 lorries proceeded to Lepugnoy for ammunition. There, 4 other of our lorries joined up. While at the station we saw a train being shunted & the points being wrong it backed into a standing train & derailing one truck in consequence. 7 lorries went to battery with ammunition. 282 company played the 7th Siege at foot-ball at Chocques, our team winning 3 goals to 1. Aeroplanes very busy indeed.

28th Another sharp frost. Church Parade at 11.30 a.m. 3 lorries went to battery with ammunition. The sergeant made us clean the lorries in the afternoon. This is against orders on a Sunday afternoon. A very cold east wind blowing. Despatch-rider Pte. (*Private*) Meek, had a serious accident on his motor-cycle in returning from the battery.

29th A very cold, wet day. Terrific wind storm in evening. Had to parade at 6.30 a.m. for a march, by the sergeants (*sergeants'*) order. Busy cleaning the lorries.

30th Aeroplanes very busy. 2 German officers passed the column in a motor car, both having been captured. The usual cleaning of lorries. The officers visited the lorries in the afternoon & inspected them & they also had a look at the dug-out we have made & were very amused at it.

1st December 1915 Usual cleaning of lorries. Pte (*Private*) Borden made a fire-place in the ground for the cooks & it acted very well. A cock (*Cockerel*) was painted on every lorry of our company, on the tail-board, as a distinction. Nothing very startling occurred.

2nd Many troops came back from the line today for a rest. At 4 p.m. 3 lorries left for Gore. When we arrived there, 3 other lorries from the company headquarters joined us, & then all lorries were loaded with the battery stores etc. At 7 p.m. the guns were removed from this position to Masingarbe. Heard that the right half battery of the 33rd Siege were coming into this position again, after having 3 weeks rest. The lorries after loading proceeded to Masingarbe & then we were sent back to our stand reaching home at 11 p.m. A very wet night. During the day there were several aeroplanes about.

3rd The 6 ammunition lorries of the right half of the battery, left Vendin & joined the company again. At 2 p.m. the 6 lorries loaded with stores proceeded to the battery, were (*where*) they were dispersed of on the way to Masingarbe, an Albion lorry, loaded with shell & driven by one of our officers, got ditched. (*Albion was a Glasgow based Motor Company and during the First World War it provided the British Army with many lorries. The Albion's were a rugged 3 ton 32 hp lorry, and like the Thornycroft and Peerless lorry's, they were a rear wheel, chain driven vehicle, after the war many of these old war-horses were converted to charabancs.)* It was one of No 1 Section lorries. The Peerless in our charge pulled it out, this being the 2nd time we had done that to-day. A Commer lorry at Chocques, which had slipped down a bank was towed out by our lorry. A dreadfully wet day. Our guns took up a new position, not very far from the left half guns at Fosse 3. We arrived back at 8.30 p.m. 3 lorries went to battery with ammunition.

4th Celebrated my birthday. Received the usual greetings from many friends. Had splendid parcels sent out. Another wet day cleaning lorries again. Football match against the 12th M.A.C. own team winning 5 goals to nil.

5th Usual 8.30 a.m. route march & afterwards cleaned lorries. Hockey match in the afternoon. 1 lorry took ammunition to the guns. Nothing of any interest to note.

6th Cleaning lorries as usual. 1 lorry took ammunition to battery. Rain all day. Football match against 47th Division Royal Engineers & our team winning 5 goals to 1. A general order that no light whatsoever was to be burning in ammunition lorries when loaded.

7th A very busy day. Pte Macgregor moved off 48 lorry to a lorry in No 4 section & Pte Buswell joined me in his place. Hockey match in the afternoon.

8th Usual parades & cleaning of lorries. Aeroplanes very active in the afternoon & they were being heavily shelled by the anti-aircraft guns. Given a half holiday to see a football match against the Royal Welsh Fusiliers, our team winning by 1 goal to nil. 2 lorries took ammunition to the battery.

9th A very wet day. Pte Heatley (Dispatch rider, ran into some lorries with his cycle & received serious injuries. This happened at Neuc le Mines (***Nouex-les-mines***). Lc.Corp (***Lance Corporal***) Gordon, another dispatch rider, fell off his machine & received injuries to his right knee. Went to rail-head for ammunition.

10th Another wet day as usual. Pte Jack tore his little finger of right hand off through wearing an aluminium ring. Taken to hospital & operated upon. Lieu (***Lieutenant***) Carlton & 2nd Lieu (***Second Lieutenant***) Cockshutt joined the company. All drivers of ammunition lorries (excepting 3rd Section) went into a billet for the winter.

11th Usual route march at 8.30 a.m. Still raining. Issued with a new tunic. At 2 p.m. left the column & proceeded to battery with ammunition. Engine went badly & water boiled twice. The Germans were shelling the vicinity of battery very heavily & 2 Jack Johnsons fell on a fosse close by. Arrived back at 6 p.m. A very wet night.

12th Usual work during the morning. In the afternoon had a half day off & went to Auchel & had a photo taken. Had a jolly good time. C. Larherety, the chief police of the town was called up by the French Government & joined the infantry. The 47th Divisional band played selections during the evening.

13th Paid 60 francs. Took lorry into work-shop to be overhauled. A very sharp frost during the night. An issue of rum after the 8.30 p.m. parade.

14th Parades & route march as usual. A very cold day. A battalion of French infantry passed through the town. 1 lorry to (**took**) ammunition to the battery. Football match in afternoon between our 1ˢᵗ team & the reserves.

15th 47ᵗʰ Division left the town & went into action. A very cold day. On guard for the 10ᵗʰ time. Half-holiday to attend the football match. Our team played the 15ᵗʰ A.S.P. (A.S.C.) & were beat by 2 goals to 1. (**15ᵀᴴ A.S.P. was an Ammunition Sub Park run by the Army Service Corps**).

16th Lieu (**Lieutenant**) Carlton took the men on a march, & was very strict, the men having to double for a considerable distance. Several batteries of artillery came into town. Things very quiet.

17th A very wet day. The fitters finished the engine & we left the shops & took our stand on the column. Issued with a new smoke helmet. Several empty lorries left the column to do work for the Royal Engineers.

18th Usual parades. The lorry tested by the fitters & found to be correct. A football match between our team & the 1ˢᵗ Artillery Ammunition Column. A very keen game resulting in our team being defeated by 2 goals to 1. The best match so far of the season.

19th Usual route march. Aeroplanes very active. Watched a German aeroplane being shelled heavily over our lines. Our team went to Neux-le-Mines to play & won 3 goals to nil. A rather heavy bombardment on part of our front. Heard that Sir J. French had resigned. (**Field Marshal Sir John French was the Commander in Chief of the BEF (British Expeditionary Forces) in Belgium and France for 18 months from August 1914 – December 1915. This controversial officer had previously been mentioned in a couple of embarrassing scandals, he was cited in the divorce of a brother officer whilst serving in India and he was also declared bankrupt. Apparently General Douglas Haig lent him a large amount of money to clear the debt and his army career was saved. After his failure at the Battle of Loos, Sir John French**

wasn't so lucky and the British Prime Minister demanded his resignation, he was replaced by his old 'friend' and adversary, Field Marshal Douglas Haig. After returning from France Sir John was made Commander in Chief of the Home Forces 1916 – 1918.)

20th Issued with a new vest. Heard that an ammunition lorry leaving Lepugnoy railhead, had been run into by a moving train whilst crossing the level-crossing & damaged the lorry very much. The drivers also severely injured.

21st Handed into stores all rifles. Issued with a bonnet cover. (**Bonnet covers were issued to conserve the heat from the engine after it had been switched off and the drivers called them either a 'Nose Bag' or the 'Tea Cosy'. During the winter periods this canvas cover was placed over the bonnet of each military vehicle to prevent frost damage to radiators, cylinders and pumps by severe frost, no such thing as anti-freeze in those days. After the petrol pump had been switched off the engine was kept running until the carburettor had been fully drained (for safety reasons) and a paraffin lamp was placed inside the engine compartment to hopefully keep the cold at bay. It was easier to maintain vehicles this way rather than draining the cooling systems, because when called into action there wouldn't have been any unfrozen water to refill the radiators.)** Half the section went to Callone Rigcourt Mine (**Probably Calonne-Ricouart-Mine**) for a hot-water bath. Heard that 2 A.S.C. drivers in yesterday's accident at level crossing had died from the injuries received. (**Please note that no actual names are recorded of these two ASC drivers on any of the Official Unit War Diary's.**) A very wet day. Much heavy firing heard in the distance.

22nd Usual route march & parades but without rifles. Went to mine for a bath which was enjoyed immensly (**immensely**). Our football team played the 6th Black Watch winning by 6 goals to nil. A half-holiday given.

23rd A very wet day. Nothing of interest to place.

24th All preparations made for Christmas day. Handed in all Ross rifles. The band of our company played carols etc round the village during the evening. 2 lorries took ammunition to the battery. Received our Xmas cards and given the privilege of sending them all off to our friends the same day.

25th Only 7.30 a.m. 8.30 a.m. & 12 oclock parades. A general holiday. At 1 oclock the whole company sat down to dinner & as is the usual custom in the army, on Xmas day the N.C.O's wait on the men. The dinner was set out in style & consisted of potatoes, peas, cold pork, apple sauce, pickles, & plum pudding. Afterwards there was plenty of beer, port wine, cigars, cigarettes etc for everybody. All had a jolly good time.

26th The sergeants had their Christmas dinner. Several men drawn for leave, it cheered all up a little, for very few have had leave up to date. In the village an awful affair occurred. About 10 a.m. a boy of about 16 pointed a loaded rifle at a domestic servant & shot her through the head. She died almost immediately.

27th Usual parades. All the N.C.O's ordered to parade for drill at 2 p.m. every day. On guard for the 11th time. A very windy night. Issued with a new Enfield rifle, No 9559.

28th Usual parades. The whole company paraded at 2 p.m. for drill. A heavy bombardment along the front. A beautiful day & aeroplanes very busy as observation was good. Went into billet to sleep.

29th Usual parades. Our team journeyed to Auchel & played the 15th A.S.P. (*Ammunition Sub Park*) the A.S.P. team winning 4 goals to 1. This team scores 3 goals in less than 9 minutes. Heavy bombardment.

30th A fine day, but nothing to mention occurred. Issued with a pair of driving gloves.

31st A very busy day. Very windy & it was very interesting to watch the aeroplanes up. One lorry went to battery with shell. Much heavy firing heard in the distance. Every one ordered to be in bed & lights out by 9 p.m. Several men in the billet were singing after 9 p.m. & the serg-major (*Sergeant-Major*) came in & ordered us to stop. A poor way of spending the last night in the year.

'1916'

1st January 1916

Usual parades. Very wet & a very strong gale blowing. Proceeded to rail-head & drew the usual quantity of ammunition. 2 Austrian cruisers sunk. The 9th Black Watch, (Battalion team) played our team in the afternoon & were given a good beating.

2nd Parades & route march as usual. A very wet day & nothing startling occurred. Heard of the sinking SS Persia. (*The S.S. Persia was a Scottish built passenger liner that was launched in 1900, tragically, and without warning, the ship was torpedoed by a German U-Boat on the 30th of December 1915 just as she was sailing off the coast of Crete. There were just over 500 passengers and crew on board and over 60% of them were killed as a result of the attack.)*

3rd Lieu (*Lieutenant*) Foot was placed on the strength of our company. N.C.O's drill at 2 p.m. The quarter-master spent the day in issuing new clothing etc to the men. I was issued with a towel. Sir Douglas Haig sent a telegram to headquarters' wishing all a Happy New Year & success in 1916.

4th Serg (*Sergeant*) Fisher took us on a route march & it was very severe for we walked about 6 miles & never halted for a rest. A beautiful day. Lieu (*Lieutenant*) Foot inspected the lorries of 3 &4 sections & found fault with almost every one. Luckily our lorry suited him.

5th Lieu (*Lieutenant*) Foot inspected the men on parade. Football match at 2 p.m., our team versus 13th Siege Battery gunners, our team scoring 4 goals to their 1. 4 men did not return from leave, missing their train in London. Several brigades of artillery went into action.

6th Nothing to note.

7th A heavy bombardment & aeroplanes very active. A very wet day. Usual parades etc.

8th 1 lorry took ammunition to the guns. Football match against the Black Watch. A very fine day. The artillery stationed near us went on a 3 days retreating march. W. Redpath went on leave.

9th A beautiful day & much heavy gun fire along the front. On guard for the 12th time. During the night there was a most terrific bombardment & we were warned to stand by (those whose lorries were loaded).

10th Heard of the evacuation of all the Allies troops from Gallipoli. Usual routine of work for the day. Several aeroplanes about. Commenced to load stones to repair our stand. (*The stand Frank is referring to is a hardstanding vehicle park where 262 Company ASC left their heavy duty vehicles when not being used.*)

11th Heavy bombardment again. Several batteries of field artillery passed through the town. Several men drawn for leave, including J. Shaw.

12th Parades etc. Big success by the French in Champagne. Heavy German losses. (*This was the Second Battle of Champagne - 25th Sept 1915 to 6th Nov 1915 and unfortunately the reality was even worse for the French. Although the Germans suffered 72,000 dead and 25,000 men taken prisoner, the French Army sustained a total of 145,000 casualties and the battle achieved absolutely nothing.*) Splendid work done by the 75" of our Allies'. 1 lorry took ammunition to battery.

13th Aeroplanes very busy indeed. Many troops moving about. Heavy firing on the front.

14th Usual parades etc. N.C.O's drill at 2 p.m. At 3 p.m. proceeded to Masingarbe (*spelt Mazingarbe by the French*) with ammunition. Left the column at 3 p.m. & arrived at 6 p.m. A beautiful day. The fitters adjusted the chains on the lorry. Heard that the 15th Division were to go into action on this day. About 30 men drew for leave.

15th Busy cleaning lorry. Several batteries of artillery passed the column. Nothing interesting occurred.

16th Cleaned lorry. Usual parades. Took a walk in the afternoon in search of an old battle field, & saw trenches which are said to have been used in 1804. (*Without confirmed dates and locations this battlefield is hard to identify, it's more than likely the area was fought over in the Napoleonic War's or was used by a French Army as a Training Ground.*) The people Marles & district go to this place in the fine weather for a picnic.

17th Usual work etc for the day. Was on guard for the 13th time. The aeroplanes were very busy as it was such a beautiful day. Had to repair a hood on a light car for the workshop staff.

18th The officer took over another billet for the men to sleep in. The men still being sent on leave & all are expecting to get it. A very heavy bombardment.

19th Cleaned lorries etc. Capt (*Captain*) Martin inspected the lorries of each section. Nothing of interest to note. Pte (*Private*) Addis awarded 3 days pack drill. During the 1st hour he turned ill & was sent to hospital.

20th Paid 40 francs. A very wet day. Prepared lorry to go on the ration job. Several got a little too much drink as it was pay day.

21st Left the column & proceeded to the battery for a week to fetch the rations etc every day. Took a load of coal from Bruay to Masingarbe. In the evening lead two load of slag from Fosse 3 to the road near the guns. Our guns very active. The Germans shelled Masingarbe.

22nd The usual run for rations etc. A very clear day & Aeroplanes very active. Several Taubes over & our aircraft guns busy firing at them. Very interesting to watch this. Masingarb(**e**) again shelled. Several killed. All the guns in this vicinity very busy. 2 load of slag lead in the evening. The people of Felistof & Vermelles ordered to remove, because they refused to billet the British troops & all estaminets put out of bounds for troops.

23rd Same work for day. Rum issue every night at battery. (***In the British Army a tot of Rum (1/16th of a pint) was given to the troops in the morning and evening if it was available. This highly desirable liquor was transported up to the trenches in 1 or 2 gallon earthenware jars that had the letters S.R.D. clearly marked on them. There are several ideas about what the letters stood for, Service Rations Depot, Supply Reserve Depot or Seldom Reaches Destination are just three. Severe weather conditions, an impending night trench raid, or a daytime stroll through no man's land were other times when it was really appreciated.***) Watched shells falling in Masingarbe about 3.30 p.m. Only slight damage done to property & no one injured. Said to be an armoured train of the Huns that comes to the front at sunset. As I was walking through the battery several shells came over close to me, one dropping about 15 yards away, but fortunately it never exploded. I got a smothering of mud.

24th Heavy bombardment by our guns. Aeroplanes very busy & were heavily shelled at times. Masingarbe again shelled. We are standing in a brewery yard & quite close to a 4.7 battery & are kept awake with them firing at night.

25th Usual work for day. The Germans sent over plenty of shells, but our batteries always reply with three times as many now. Watched a battery of

4.7" guns firing. Enemy aeroplanes very active & were heavily shelled by our aircraft guns. In the evening lead two loads of stones for the battery position.

26th Same work for day. Fine weather. Had a look round the B.E.F's canteen in Bethune & formed a very good opinion of it. Enemy aeroplane over our lines & dropped several bombs near Fosse 3. Big attack by the Germans at night but repulsed. Our guns very busy.

27th Usual work for day. At Bethune the contact breaker on magneto broke & we were stopped for rest of the day. No. 12 lorry towed our lorry to Neoux-le-Mines to our caterpillars & we stayed there for the night & the above lorry finished our work. Another big attack by the Germans but unsuccessful.

28th The fitters came from the column & repaired magneto. The brigade headquarters lorry did our work for the day. Several shells dropped in Masingarbe, but did little damage. Returned to the column after a very hard week's work. In the morning a shell came over & dropped in the mine, bursting a water-main. We were only stood about 20 yds (*yards*) away & were very lucky to escape.

29th The usual 8.30 am parade. After the route march commenced to get the mud off the lorry. Several went on leave. In the afternoon our team played the 25th Brigade R.F.A. (*Royal Field Artillery*) at football. A very exciting match & our team were giving a good beating, the R.F.A. winning 3 goals to 1.

30th Very busy cleaning lorry etc. Usual half-holiday. A very heavy bombardment on the front. Zeppelin raid on Paris.

31st No 3 section lorries took up a new position near the church in Marles. Fetched a load of stone from Bruay to repair the position. Heavy bombardment at the front & several lorries from the column took up ammunition. Hockey match against the 25th Brigade R.F.A. our team winning. Issued with waterproof capes.

1st February 1916 Usual parades & cleaning lorries constituted our work for the day. At 2 p.m. had an hours' rifle drill. Several lorries took ammunition to the guns & much heavy firing heard at the front. Zeppelin raid on the East coast. Many killed & injured. (***Many places, both large and small, were bombed by Zeppelins during the Great War, from Edinburgh in Scotland down to London and places like Hull, King's Lynn and Lowestoft in-between. The effect and damage to the war industry was negligible and the raids only stirred up more belligerence for the German nation.***)

2nd Same work for day & half-holiday given. Our team played 256 A.S.C. at Vendin & got defeated. Result 6 goals to nil. Many troops passed through the town including a regiment of French infantry-men.

3rd Usual routine of work. At 2 p.m. paraded with smoke helmets for inspection by the section officers. I was issued with a new one, one being defective. All lorries issued with bonnet covers & a crow bar. At 4 p.m. went to Mine 3 at Bruay for a bath which was very acceptable.

4th Usual parades etc. At 11 a.m. the Mechanical Transport's Inspector from General Headquarters paid us a surprise visit. He inspected several lorries & all was satisfactory. In the afternoon he inspected the caterpillars. Paid 20 francs.

5th On guard for the 14th time. Busy cleaning lorries. Half-holiday given. Battalion of Dublin Fusiliers billeted here for the night. 12 men went on leave.

6th A very wet, cold day. Boxing match at Vendin promoted by the C.O. of 256 company. The officers & all men of our company subscribed £2 towards the Commercial Motor Comfort's Fund.

7th Took lorry into workshop to have towing hooks fitted to chassis. A very wet day. Rifle drill at 2 p.m.

8th Busy carting slag from Bruay to repair the position. A battalion of Munster Fusiliers passed through the town.

9th Nothing of any interest to note.

10th Usual parades etc. Busy cleaning lorries. Lieu (*Lieutenant*) Young commenced to test the petrol consumption of the Thornycroft lorries.

11th A very fine day. The Daimler petrol store lorry was changed over to No 3 section, as an ammunition lorry, in place of one of the old Thornycroft's, No 51 lorry made a gun store lorry. (*If the transmission, chassis and engine of a lorry had been worked to the point of non-serviceability, then it was often used at an ASC base for storage reasons.*)

12th At 2 p.m. our team played 256 Comp football. This was the 4th match with this company & our team won 1 goal to nil. The ground was very wet. It was a most excitable game.

13th The usual half-holiday. 1 lorry took up ammunition to battery. Was on guard for the 15th time & very wet windy night. My 1st wet night on guard since joining.

14th At 10 a.m. went to Auchel for a load of coal for the billets etc. Very windy day. Heard that the Germans were attacking heavily on the Western front, but without success.

15th The usual parades. Lieu (**Lieutenant**) Foot on the 8.30 a.m. parade marched us off for drill etc. Almost too windy to hear the orders.

16th No parades as it was such a wet day. Nothing particular occurred.

17th A very wet busy day. Our team played the 6th Brigade R.G.A. (**Royal Garrison Artillery**) & won quite easily. Still much wind but the roads are drying a little.

18th Paid 20 francs. Raining as usual. Heard of a big Russian success & that the Turkish fortress called Ezeroum (**Erzurum**) had fallen & the Russians had taken it. A brigade of artillery came into the town & stayed the night. (**The Erzurum Offensive 10 Jan – 16 Feb 1916 ended with the Russian Army capturing the strategic City of Erzurum from the Ottoman (Turkish) Empire. This undermanned city was only captured because the majority of its best Turkish troops, and weaponry, had been diverted to Gallipoli in 1915 to repel Churchill's attack on the 'German soft underbelly'. The Russians lost 1,000 men Killed in Action, 4,000 wounded and they also suffered with 4,000 cases of frost-bite. The Turks lost 10,000 men who were killed and wounded and another 5,000 were taken prisoner.)**

19th Usual parades & cleaning lorries. At 2 p.m. the Colonel of our Brigade & Major Moberly inspected our lorries & found great satisfaction all round. Our team played the 15th A.P.P. & won.

20th A beautiful day after a severe night's frost. Lieu (**Lieutenant**) Foot (orderly officer for day) had us drilling after the 8.30 a.m. parade. This has never been the case before on a sunday (**Sunday**) morning. No's 1 & 2 sections played 3 & 4 sections football, the latter winning 4 to 1. About 2 p.m. a squadron of aeroplanes (about 25 in number) were seen flying in the direction of the German lines, & most likely carrying out a raid. A very fine night.

21st Usual parades. A fine day. At 1 p.m. a heavy bombardment by the British & French & continued until dark. 3 lorries took up shell at 6 p.m.

22nd About 7 a.m. commenced to snow & continued all day. Several lorries went to railhead for ammunition. No 4 section took up a new stand near the church. At 5 p.m. orders came through that all ammunition in the column to be taken to the respective batteries. A severe frost.

23rd No parades as it was snowing too much. At 2 p.m. the Headquarters played the Workshop football & the latter won 5 goals to 1. The ground was thick with snow & most unfavourable for the game. About 12 lorries took up ammunition. Very bad travelling. A sharp frost. Rum issue.

24th About 12 lorries went to railhead for ammunition. I was one of a party told off to load lorries. Snow again & now it is about 6" deep. Paraded at 10 a.m. with respirators. 18 men left the column.

25th No parades again. Still snowing. Several lorries again went to battery we are very busy. On guard at 6 p.m. & snowing as usual & it was no desirable job. 16th time on guard.

26th Commenced to thaw. Football match at 2 p.m. between Workshops & the 19th Siege A.S.C. men the latter losing. Went to battery with 46 lorry as the driver (J W. Shaw) was playing in the match. Arrived back at 6 p.m. Rum issue after the 8.30 p.m. parade.

27th A section of a 6" battery arrived in the town & stayed the night, before proceeding into action, at some place unknown. The 2nd Division Field Artillery are billeted around here for a time. A cold wet day. Heard of the big German offensive around Verdun. (*The Battle of Verdun: 21 Feb 1916 – 20 Dec 1916. Verdun is a sacrosanct medieval French citadel that is situated about 150 miles east of Paris, the Germans changed their tactics when they tried to capture the impregnable Forts at Verdun. The German Storm Troopers were issued with flame-throwers for the first time and they only carried automatic weapons and hand-grenades to carry out this initial attack. Over the next 9* months, 3 weeks and 6 days the French sustained just over ½ a million casualties and the Germans didn't fare much better. *Authors note: Some 'English' friends of mine have stated quite categorically that they would never visit the Verdun Battlefield because it was 'only' the French who fought there. Underneath the Verdun Ossuary there are the remains of 130,000 French soldiers who perished defending Verdun and 15,000 more are buried outside. It is only when you visit Verdun that you can fully understand what is meant by the phrase, 'Nearly bled France dry'.)*

28th Orders published to the effect that no oil or petrol was to be used for cleaning lorries & any driver losing a petrol can, or even stopper, would be charged 2 frs 40c & no man to clean his hands or arms with petrol. The artillery left the town. (*By 1916 the UK Government was funding the entire British Empires' war disbursement as well as supporting the Italian and Russian struggles. The British Army started implementing minor restrictions on its own troops to try and cut down this massive expenditure, a lot of Two Francs and Forty Centimes would eventually add up into thousands of Pounds.*)

29th Usual parades & route march. At 2 p.m. team played the 6th Siege Battery. Result draw. 4 German aeroplanes seen over our lines, subject to heavy shell fire & eventually I (*it*) was to be seen descending very quickly over Bethune direction from here. The 10th Northumberland Fusiliers came into town for the night. Met with several Hull men & had a jolly good time. Issued with a new smoke helmet & gave into store the old one. Beautiful day.

1st March 1916 Usual parades etc. At 2 p.m. our team played the Northumberland Fusiliers & won 6 goals to 2. Half holiday given. Heard that 2 German captive observation balloons had broken loose & passed over the Western front at a great high & travelling very fast, going westward.

2nd Route march etc at 8.30 a.m. Every man issued with a blue dungaree suit & orders published to the effect that they were to always be worn on working parades (*These blue dungaree's were issued for use when carrying out* *routine maintenance on vehicles, they protected the drivers uniforms from oil and petrol stains and excessive wear and tear*). This order to be strictly obeyed. 2 German aeroplanes over our lines. Both passed over here. Our machines gave chase & it was a fine sight. Heard they dropped 2 bombs in Auchel & did some damage.

3rd A very busy day. At 11 a.m. left the column & proceeded to the battery for a week to do the ration work, calling at Bruay, on the way there for coal. A wet day. At 4 p.m. the Germans commenced to shell our lines very heavily, preparatory to an attack. Our field battery were busy firing all night.

4th Snowy all day & roads very bad & much wet about. Did the usual run for rations etc. Pay day at the column, unfortunately I was given a miss. With the heavy downfall of snow the German attack did not take place. They sent several shells over & shrapnel during the afternoon.

5th Usual run for rations etc but a bit more exciting. While in Bethune at the station, a Taube came over, at a great height, & dropped 3 bombs. One fell in a field, outside the town, near a Supply Transport Column. During the morning the Germans sent over about 60 shells near a battery. Very little damage done, & only two men slightly wounded. One fell on the road to the foss (*fosse*) & prevented us getting up with lorry. At night we filled it in with bricks.

6th Same work again for the day. Snowing all day & very bad travelling. Our artillery very active all night along the front. Lieu (**Lieutenant**) Randall joined the unit.

7th Snowing again. Usual run for rations. Nothing interesting to note. Lieu (**Lieutenant**) Randall came at 7 p.m. to pay me as I was not paid on the 4th, being away from the column. A very quiet night on the front, scarcely a shot to be heard. Parcel from home.

8th Usual work for day. Taubes were over our lines several times during the day. At night the artillery were very active on both fronts & it was some bombardment. Heard that the French were still favourably situated at Verdun. Visited the B.E.F. canteen in Bethune & formed a very good opinion of it.

9th Still snowing. Usual work. Car broke down. Several taubes came over our lines. Heard that Germany had declared war on Portugal. (*The British Government demanded that Portugal confiscate numerous German and Austro-Hungarian ships that were docked in its ports. As a result of the Portuguese compliance with this 'request', on the 9th March 1916 Germany declared war on what was up to then, a neutral Portugal. The Portuguese Government responded the next day and declared war on Germany and its army eventually deployed and fought at Neuve-Chappelle in France.*) A Taube over Marles-le-Mines & dropped 2 bombs but doing no damage. A colonel inspected the lorries.

10th More snow & a very cold day. Our artillery very active. Same work for day & at 4 p.m. left Masingarbe & returned to column after a hard week's work. The Dublin Fusiliers came into the town.

11th Busy washing lorry at the river. Football match at 2 p.m. against the Fusiliers but our team won quite easily. All German attacks at Verdun completely failed so far. (*The German General, Erich Von Falkenhayn, had made some minor gains at Verdun by this time but by the end of March 1916 he had suffered nearly 81,000 casualties.*) The police raided several estaminets & found soldiers drinking coffee & rum & some gambling. Both are strictly forbidden & all so caught were put under open arrest.

12th A nice day & half holiday. The church parade at 10 a.m. of the Fusiliers was a fine sight, attending at the R.C. church in village.

13th Busy cleaning lorry. Usual parades & rifle drill at 2 p.m. At 1 p.m. a Taube was over here & dropped a newspaper "The French Gazette" giving a list of all

French soldiers wounded & prisoners of war in Germany. (**The "French Gazette" ceased publishing in 1915 after Germany had invaded France and Belgium, so this must have been an old copy.**) This is a rather strange incident. The inhabitants here ordered to have all lights out at 8 p.m. & not to be out in the street after that time. The men caught gambling etc paraded before the O.C. but all were let off.

14th Cleaning lorry etc. A very nice day. The drum & fife & bugle band of the fusiliers paraded the town from 5 to 6 p.m. A fine sight. Aeroplanes very busy.

15th Usual work for day. Lieu (**Lieutenant**) Randall orderly officer for the day & he put us through the drills directly after the 8.30 a.m. parade. Section officers inspected all tool kits at 10 a.m. At 9.30 p.m. after every one had nicely got to bed a Taube fly (**flew**) over & dropped two bombs in this vicinity. It was such a fine moonlight night. Heavy artillery very active at the front. The 13th Siege moved two of their guns.

16th Fine day. Usual parades & work. Nothing important to note today.

17th St Patrick's Day & a very nice day too. The Dublin Fusiliers attended church in the morning & at 2.30 p.m. sports were held. A very good entry & a most enjoyable afternoon was spent. Given a half holiday. The chief events were, ¼, 1 & 3 mile flat races, cycle race, mule race, dancing, erecting wire entanglement, machine gun firing, bomb throwing, tug of war & the band of the battalion playing selections at intervals. A very good attendance. General Munro, & many other distinguished officers were present. (**Previously, General Munro had taken over the 'flawed' Gallipoli campaign from the 'flawed' General Sir Ian Hamilton in 1915, General Munro personally ordered and commanded the Commonwealth withdrawal from Gallipoli.**)

18th Usual parades etc. At 2 p.m. our men played the Dublin Fusiliers at hockey & won 3 goals to nil. The Germans heavily bombarded Masingarbe during the day. A gunner at our battery was hit by a fragment of shell &

received most serious wounds & died almost immediately. He is buried quite close to one of the guns. (*Sadly this Gunner isn't mentioned by name in any of the War Diaries I've searched*) Paid 20 francs.

19th A fine day. Usual parades etc, also rifle drill. At 10.15 a.m. paraded, & proceeded to a C.E. service, held in the town school. A heavy bombardment during the day & aeroplanes were very active. 2 lorries loaded with ammunition & they proceeded to the battery at 3 p.m. These lorries brought back several charge cases, which had accidentally caught fire by shrapnel bursting overhead. The band of the Dublin's paraded the town in the evening.

20th Usual work & parades. Much heavy firing heard at the front.

22nd A very busy day. Raining most of the day. During the afternoon an explosion occurred somewhere near the village.

23rd Usual parades etc. Half holiday given. 2 lorries took up ammunition. Football match with the Fusiliers. Aeroplanes very active & a taube over this district.

24th On getting up, found it had been snowing all the night. No work done too busy keeping warm & much fun snowballing. Nothing interesting occurred. Much snow again & very cold. Rum issued at night.

25th On guard for the 17th time & very cold. At 3 p.m. we had orders given to call up all Daimler drivers to empty the water out of engines. This caused much excitement. (*During World War 1 Daimler was a Coventry based British Motor Vehicle Company that produced the 40 hp 3 ton lorry for the British Army, the Company also became involved in producing aircraft engines, artillery tractors, tank engines and the firm also produced shell casings for the Royal Artillery.*)

26th Snowing again & much wet & very cold. Inspection of lorries by section officers at 10 a.m. Started lorry up & caught fire. Football match at 2 p.m. between the 19th & 13th A.S.C. men.

27th Usual parades etc. Church Parade for the R.C.'s. The Dublin's went into action & the Argyle & Sutherland Highlanders came & took over their billets. Half holiday given. Several men went on leave which has commenced once more. Issued with a new pair of boots.

28th Orders to the effect that all men had at all times to wear both respirators. 14 lorries of 256 Company came to Marles & were joined to our company.

29th A beautiful day & aeroplanes very active. Several taubes over our lines & were heavily fired on. Heard that the British front had been lengthened & we had taken over all positions from the French as far south as the Somme. News to the effect that the French were favourably situated at Verdun. (*The French had recently repulsed a German attack and regained part of Avocourt Wood in Verdun*) Lieu (*Lieutenant*) Glossop joined the unit & Capt (*Captain*) Martin took over command of a new column. All sorry to hear he was leaving.

30th At 7 a.m. left the column with several other lorries to do work for the R.E. (*Royal Engineers*) & proceeded to Verquineoul (*Verquigneul*) & load stones to repair roads at Sally Labourse (*Sailly-Labourse*). A fine day & roads very dusty. Our aeroplanes very busy along the front. Arrived back at column at 4 p.m.

31st At 9 a.m. proceeded to Masingarbe with 1 other lorry & brought back to column the gun platforms. While at Masingarbe 2 Taubes came over & several shells were falling in this vicinity. Several lorries out on Engineers work. Guard to fall in in the future without overcoats.

1st April 1916 Usual parades etc & busy cleaning lorry. Football match between the A & S.H (*Argyle &Sutherland Highlanders*) & our team. We won by 2 goals to nil. A very fine match & many spectators there. The battalion pipes attended & paraded during half-time.

2nd At 7 a.m. went on R.E's work with 6 other lorries. Took one load of stone from Verquineoul (**Verquigneul**) to Berbur (**Burbure**) near Lillers & returned to column at 1.30 p.m. A very hot day. Half holiday given.

3rd Usual parades etc & busy with cleaning lorries. At 10 a.m. section officers inspected all tool kits. G Lydenham put in charge of clothing store lorry. After 8.30 p.m. there was an issue of rum. A heavy bombardment along the line.

4th Parades etc & paid 20 francs. A very dull day & inclined to rain. Heard of 2 zeppelin raids on England & one had been bought down in the Thames estury (**estuary**). (**L-15 was just one of five airships that were on a bombing raid of London on the 1st April 1916, 28 civilians had been killed and 44 wounded as a result of the raid. Zeppelin L-15 had been riddled by British anti-aircraft fire from an Artillery Battery based in Purfleet in Essex. L-15's superstructure and back had been broken and the wreckage fell into the mouth of the Thames just off the coast of Margate. One member of the airship drowned in the Thames and the others were rescued by a British armed trawler.**)

5th A very busy day. At 2.30 p.m. Pte's (**Private's**) Ducker & Henderson, who had challenged each other, ran a 120 yds (**Yards**) flat race, the first named winning. At 6 p.m. saw a cockfight at the sergent's (**sergeant's**) mess, between a cock belonging our company & a Frenchman's. Our cock was the winner. This is a very cruel sport, but a great sport in this country. Generally held on a sunday (**Sunday**). (**Cock fighting was banned in England, Wales and all British Overseas Territories under the Cruelty to Animals Act of 1835, Scotland followed suit in 1895 and therefore it was illegal for any soldier serving in the British Army to attend these meetings during the First World War.**)

6th Usual parades & work for day. A dull & cold day too. Nothing interesting to note. Was on guard for the 15th time. Several lorries on engineers work.

7th Left the column with 7 other lorries at 7 a.m. & proceeded to Noeux-le-Mines on engineers work & arrived back at 4.30 p.m. A very cold day. Pte (*Private*) Brunwin left the column for London, going to take a commission. He was given a hearty send off & we are all sorry to lose him. (*By 1916 the British Army had lost a lot of subalterns because each patrol and attack was nearly always led by either a 2nd Lieutenant or Lieutenant, which gave them an increased chance of getting either injured or killed. To replace these Officers the more experienced and gifted NCO's and Privates were offered the chance of becoming a commissioned Officer. At the start of the war the average age of a Battalion Commander was over 50, by 1917 he was just 28 years old. Captain Anthony Eden of the Kings Royal Rifle Corps, and later British Prime-Minister, became his Battalions' Adjutant at the age of 18 years old and a Breveted Brigade Major at the young age of 20 years old.)* Bathing parade at 1 p.m.

8th Lieu (*Lieutenant*) Rendal on parade & marched down to the football field for drill. A very nice day. Many aeroplanes about as observation very good. Several lorries on Engineers work & on returning to the column No 47 lorry driven by Pte. (*Private*) Bourdon ran over & killed almost immediately a little boy 4 years old. Lieu (*Lieutenant*) Glossop inspected the lorries.

9th Usual parades & work. A subscription got up for the parents of the little boy killed yesterday. 256 Company played our company football & won 3 goals to 1. Another cock fight held at an estaminet in the village, our cock being so severely injured that he was killed. Name taken for going on leave.

10th At 7 a.m. left the column with 7 other lorries & proceeded to Noeux-le-Mines to load slag for the Engineers. Whilst there a bomb was dropped near the station from a Taube & a shell from our aircraft guns came down & nearly hit an A.S.C. private. It did not burst. Just as we were leaving, the Germans commenced to shell the town. They did this from 5 a.m. to about 6 p.m. yesterday continually & some houses were damaged, & several of our soldier's killed & wounded.

11th Usual parades etc. At 9 a.m. the little boy, killed by one of our lorries, was buried. All the Roman Catholics attended the funeral, belonging to this column & 4 acted as bearers. A wet day & busy preparing lorry for next journey. At 1 p.m. paraded & marched to the baths. 1 lorry took up ammunition to the guns.

12th At 7 a.m. went on Engineer's work again. A very cold & wet day. Published that the total subscriptions for the parents of the boy killed totalled 310 francs (**Over £3,000 in today's money**). Arrived back at column at 4.30 p.m.

13th Usual parades & work (cleaning lorry). Leave stopped & all men recalled from home. Another wet & cold day.

14th At 10 a.m. left the column & proceeded to battery to fetch the rations daily for one week. Called at Bruay for coal. A very wet, cold night & all very quiet on the front.

15th Run for rations to Noeux-le-Mines etc. A cold day. The Arras, Noeux-le-Mines road heavily shelled by the Germans & saw several shells fall in a mine on the road. At 3 p.m. our football team visited the battery & played on land near FOSSE 3; the battery team winning 1 goal to nil. During the night the Germans attacked on this front without success. During the night 2 Taubs came over & dropped bombs on Noeux-le-Mines. It was a beautiful moonlight night.

16th On leaving the battery front spring on near side broke in two & we were prevented from fetching the rations. About 11 a.m. the Germans shelled this part very heavily, several dropping on the fosse. A shell dropped on the sergent's (**sergeant's**) dugout, but luckily no one was hurt. Another fell near a French cart & badly damaged it. During the day aeroplanes were very active & I saw 2 attacks made by our aviators on the German aviators. Our guns fired several rounds.

17th A very cold & wet day. The usual run for rations. About 4 p.m. the Germans shelled Masingarbe & several shrapnel shells burst over here. A very windy day & no aeroplanes up.

18th Raining all day & very cold. Paid 20 francs. Nothing much to note, the usual artillery activity along the line. Took the french (**French**) cart damaged by a shell to the salvage.

19th Another cold, wet day, with much wind. The usual run for rations. Artillery very active during the night. A terrible wet night too.

20th The usual run for day. The right-half battery fired 50 rounds. 1 Caterpillar was transferred to another company. At dusk removed the office from Felistoffe to Masingarbe.

21st Good Friday. The usual run for rations etc. The Germans shelled the fosse very heavily about breakfast time 8 a.m. & we had to take cover & get into a dugout. Several Taubes over at the time & it was pretty hot for about an hour. Returned to the column at night. A very wet night.

22nd A terribly wet day & busy washing lorry. At 10 a.m. the M.T. (Motor Transport) general inspected the column, & found fault with several things, which were to be rectified by (**the time**) he paid his next visit, on the 25th. This made us all very busy. The address of company altered & it was made into headquarters of the 1st Corps Heavy Artillery.

23rd A beautiful day. Busy cleaning lorry. Another workshop added to the column. Half-holiday given. Heavy bombardment on the front & aeroplanes very busy. Several lorries took up ammunition.

24th Usual parades & work. Half-holiday given & the whole company were photographed in a group in the afternoon. Orders to the effect at (**that**) in the future a day guard to mount at 7 a.m. until 6 p.m. without rifles in the future

25th A very busy day. All men in the company on fatigue, squaring the place up for the general inspection. A hot day & had a hard days work.

26th In future Wednesday and Saturday afternoon's were to be recognised half holidays. The usual parades & work for day. During the night of the 25th a Taube flew over here about 10 p.m. 7 dropped 2 bombs near Auchel. At 3 p.m. we were called out along with 4 other lorries to take ammunition to the battery. On the way there, on passing the fosse in Nouex-le-Mines, the Germans sent over several shells, which dropped on top of the fosse. Our battery were firing from 9 a.m. to dusk. Arrived back at 10 p.m. Heavy bombardment & the Germans attacked & took some trenches from us near Morocco. Leave commenced.

27th Usual parades & work. A very hot day. In future we are an ammunition lorry again. A heavy bombardment on & 6 lorries took up ammunition. Lieu (**Lieutenant**) Young paid us 16 francs (Canteen funds). The Scots went up to the trenches. & the Fusilier's took over their billets.

28th Proceeded to Bethune at 7 a.m. along with 9 other lorries to remove wood for the Engineers. Saw a private attempt suicide by jumping into the canal. The Germans very active on this front & gas used by them. Many wounded & men gassed coming front (**from**) the front in ambulances. Arrived back at 5 p.m. A fine day. The Germans shelled a horse line in Beavry (**Beuvry**).

29th Usual parades & work. The 9th Battalion Royal Fusiliers came into the village for a rest. The Germans bombarded our lines & attacked but without success. At 6 p.m. all men were medically examined. Ordered to stand by in case ammunition was wanted. Usual work & parades for day.

30th This column made H.Q. of a Siege Park for the 1st Corps Heavy Artillery. Several lorries from other batteries came under our O.C.'s command. Heavy bombardment along the front by our guns & 4 lorries took up shell. On guard for the 19th time.

1st May 1916 Parades etc & same work for day. During the night we bombarded the German lines very heavily. The 13th Siege (Ammo Col) left the column & went to Bruay.

2nd Proceeded to Bethune at 7 a.m. on Engineers work. Went to Lillars along with 4 other lorries for material. Arrived back at 5 p.m. Thunderstorm crossed over here.

3rd Usual work for day very hot. 4 lorries took up ammunition. At 1 p.m. went to the baths. At 6.15 p.m. all units paraded for church service. A chaplain appointed for the 1st Corps.

4th Parades etc for day. Heavy firing along the front. Aeroplanes very busy. Reported loss of another zeppelin. Paid 20 francs.

5th At 10 p.m. proceeded to Masingarbe with J. Shaw on 46 lorry. A fine day & artillery very active on both sides. The left half of 13th Siege Battery went to Vendin. A new 8" gun arrived & was brought up to Masingarbe for trial under our Major.

6th Usual parades etc. A very hot day. No 3 section lorries took over a new stand. Heard that General Townsend had surrendered to the Turks at Kut. Usual half holiday. (*Siege of Kut Mesopotamia (modern Iraq) 7th December 1915 – 29th April 1916. At the end of the siege General Charles Townsend surrendered over 13,000 of his British and Indian troops who were marched off into Turkish captivity, whilst the General saw out the rest of the war in* *relative luxury on the island of Heybeliada, over 50% of his men who had been taken prisoner died from disease or at the hands of their captors.*)

7th At 7.a.m. proceeded to Bethune with J.S. (***Private J Shaw?***) on 46 lorry on engineers work. Went to Lillers for material. A wet afternoon. 1 lorry took up shell.

8th Several lorries went out on engineer work. Stood by in case I went on leave. At 6 p.m. given pass & paid 80 francs & proceeded to Lepugnoy. (***80 Francs would have equated to over £200 in today's money.***)

9th and 10th Left at 1.30 p.m. by the leave train & arrived Boulogne 9.30 a.m. Marched to rest camp & returned at 12.30 a.m. & embarked for Folkstone on S.S. Victor at 2 p.m. Arrived Folkestone 4 p.m. London 7 p.m. Hull 5 a.m. on the 10th. A very tiring journey. Wet all day 9th.

11th May 1916 Home on leave.

12th May 1916

13th May 1916

14th May 1916 Went to Cadbury & called on schoolmaster.

15th Left home at 11.25 p.m. for London. Arrived London 6 a.m. on the 16th.

16th Arrived Folkestone 10.30 a.m. Embarked on S.S. London for Bologne (***Boulogne***) at 11 a.m. & arrived 12.30 a.m. Marched to rest camp for night. A rough place to stay at. (***See 27th May 1915***)

17th Paraded at 6 a.m. Dodged all fatigues. Marched to station at 11.15 a.m. & left here at 2 p.m. arriving back at Lepugnoy at 8 p.m. & glad to get back to unit.

18th Usual parades etc. Heard that the column had been very busy during the past week. That Serg (**Sergeant**) Sykes, Corp (**Corporal**) Pullen & several men of 13th Siege had been wounded. That fur coats & 1 blanket had been given in. That B Workshop had left the Park for St Omer under the charge of Lieu (**Lieutenant**) Cockshutt. At 7 p.m. 12 lorries proceeded to Fosse 3, to move the 2 guns, to a new position near Fosse 2. A quiet night along the line. Arrived back in the early morning about 4.30 a.m.

19th Slept until 12 noon & prepared lorry for next journey. Heavy firing along the front. A very hot day & aeroplanes very active, several combats taking place along the front. On guard for the 20th time & without an overcoat. During the night aeroplanes were over here practicing flying at night & they were lit up with electric lights & it was a fine sight.

20th Usual parades etc. Busy preparing lorry for next journey. A very hot day. At 7 p.m. 12 lorries left here for the battery, (Fosse 2) to move the 2 left-half guns. The French authorities owning this mine objected to the guns being situated here. They were moved to Bully Grenay, into a brickyard. 3 lorries got ditched. Very quiet on the front. Arrived back at 2 a.m. & Lieu (**Lieutenant**) Young gave orders for all men to be on the 8.30 a.m. parade.

21st A very hot day. The Germans attacked on this front. Several lorries took up ammunition. The ration lorry at the guns was hit by shrapnel in several places & one of the ammunition lorries too. No 1 gun fired a shell which burst directly it left the gun. Gun not damaged, but wounded 3 gunners rather badly. The Germans bombarded our front heavily & sent over much shrapnel.

22nd Parades etc for day & usual work. 2 lorries took up ammunition. The 8th Royal Fusiliers left here & the Suffolks took over their billets in the village. Several aeroplanes went over the German lines on a raid.

23rd Orders to parade in future at 7 a.m. (Roll call) & proceed for ½ hrs sharp walk. The 8.30 a.m. route march cancelled & the 8.30 p.m. roll-call parade to be near each unit. The Suffolks came into the town & took over the R.F.'s (*Royal Fusiliers*) billets. A very hot day.

24th A very hot day & very busy. Took lorry into workshop to have a new bush & gudgeon pin fitted, on 2nd cylinder. At 6.15 p.m. attended church service. A heavy bombardment on this front. Germans attacking heavily.

25th A heavy shower in the morning. Engine finished & tested. 2 men of the Suffolks killed & 2 severely injured by bomb throwing, whilst drilling on the parade ground here.

26th At 7 a.m. proceeded to Bethune along with 9 other lorries on 1st Corps Engineers work & arrived back at 4 p.m. Orders that all men on leaving the park to be properly dressed, (belts & puttees). Military police to see this is carried out. Serg (*Sergeant*) Cornwall posted to the Base.

27th A very fine day. Heavy artillery fire along the front. Heard that another of 9.2 guns of the 13th Siege Battery had burst whilst firing & that 5 of the Gunners had been instantly killed. At 2.30 p.m. paraded & proceeded to the baths. Several lorries took up ammunition to the respective batteries.

28th Usual work cleaning lorries & section officers inspected same during morning. Orders that smoking hereafter strictly prohibited whilst working on, or driving lorry. The 7th Suffolks left here. Pte (*Private*) C. G. Scott promoted Lance Corporal. Several aeroplanes went out together & no doubt proceeding on a raid over the German lines. Confirmation at this church. Issued with kakhi (*Khaki*) overcoat.

29th At 7 a.m. proceeded to Bethune along with several other lorries on engineers work. During the morning the Germans shelled the mine at

Annequin heavily & I saw several burst, also they sent over much high explosive shrapnel before the village of Beuvry & Annequin. Whilst at Sally Laborse I saw several of our aeroplanes being fired on by the enemy. Several lorries took up ammunition.

30th During the night there was much rain. Busy cleaning lorry & touched same up with paint in places. Confirmation at the R.C. church here by the bishop. A very impressive sight. Heavy bombardment during the night. The 9 th R.F.'s (*Royal Fusiliers*) returned to here.

31st At 7 a.m. paraded & told off for police duty until 6 p.m. At 6.15 p.m. Church Parade. A beautiful day. Several lorries took up shell. A body of cavalry passed through the town. A workshop (256 Comp) joined up the Park & a corporal attached to same put under arrest for being drunk & disorderly.

1st June 1916 Usual parades & sharp march. Helped to take off tyres on 49 Peerless. On guard for the 21st time. Several lorries took up ammunition & an intense bombardment along the front. Germans still attacking heavily on Verdun.

2nd A fine day. Lorries on engineers work & so many took up ammunition. New canteen built. A great improvement on the old. At 11 p.m. called up after getting to bed & proceeded along with 1 other lorry to railhead for shell. Took up 30 rounds on each lorry to Fosse 3. No 1 gun moved from Masingarbe to old position at the fosse to fire on a special target. Got back to the column at 3.30 a.m. next morning. A quiet night along the front.

3rd Turned out about 11 a.m. & prepared lorry for next journey. Half holiday. Football match in the afternoon. Heard of a great naval battle in the North Sea. (*Very likely to be the Battle of Jutland – 31st May to 1st June 1916*) A very hot day. Nothing important to note.

4th Parades etc as usual. Handed in waterproof capes. Paid 20 francs at 2 p.m. by Lieu (*Lieutenant*) Farmer. Orders that after 6 p.m. all ranks to wear puttees and belts in billeting area after 6 p.m. The 10th Siege left this park & proceeded to an unknown destination; 4 days journey away. 20 lorries on engineer work.

5th A very strong wind & the weather unfavourable for flying. Usual work for day. 1 lorry took up ammunition & several lorries on Engineers work. Further news of great Naval Battle, the Germans calculated to have lost 22 ships & the British 14. (*The reality was somewhat different to the news that Frank had been given – 14 Royal Navy ships had actually been sunk with 6,094 Royal Navy sailors killed against 11 German ships sunk and 2,551 German sailors killed.*)

6th Usual work for day. Raining all day. Rumours that our battery was re-removing. News received of a great Russian victory against the Austrians, capturing 13,000 prisoners. The Germans attacked heavily near Ypres, & the Canadians did splendid fighting again.

7th Busy working on lorries. Official news received here that Lord Kitchener & his staff had been sunk, whilst on a journey to Russia on the (*HMS*) Hampshire, near the Orkneys. (*On 5th June 1916 Field Marshal Lord Kitchener was travelling to Russia on a diplomatic mission when the ship he was travelling on struck a mine that had been laid by a German U-Boat.*) Another Russian success, capturing 25,000 prisoners, 100 cannon & 60 machine-guns. Church parade at 6.15 p.m. Football match our team playing the 8th Royal Fusiliers.

8th Fine day. The 8th Royal Fusiliers left here & went to the front & 7th Suffolks took over their billets. The left half of battery came out of action & proceeded to a place not known to us. The lorries accompanied the guns. Went to Labuissiere (*Bruay-la-Buissiere*) for petrol. Tunic issued.

9th Went to Labussiere for petrol etc & took to the left half who halted at a village called Duval (*probably Dieval*) near St Pol (*probably Saint-Pol-sur-Ternoise*). In the afternoon took off both back wheels & tyres off same. The Russians reported captured many prisoners & have took luck. (*The battles of Luck were a Russian Summer Offensive which were more commonly known in Russia as Lutsk.*)

10th Wheels sent to tyre press to have new tyres fitted. During the afternoon put on wheels again & made ready for the road. A heavy thunderstorm, with hailstones. A workshop sent from Siege Park to the base at St Omer. Issued with blue-overalls.

11th Another heavy thunder storm during afternoon. The 49th Siege Battery moved to a position further south. Usual work for day. On guard at night for 22nd time. Lorry loaded with gun-stores etc.

12th A very wet day. At 3 p.m. proceeded to rail-head with 3 other lorries for ammunition. At 6 p.m. went to battery (Masingarbe) 1 lorry & 3 to Bully grenay. Arrived back at 9 p.m. Had a good look at the latest type of 8" howitzer gun which our battery are experimenting with. Informed that it was a very good gun. A quiet night on this front. (*The experimental 8" howitzer gun was made using some shortened and bored out naval barrels that were deemed to be redundant by the Royal Navy, although the trial was judged to be a success there were some shortcomings. The weapon was very heavy, unreliable and suffered from premature explosions, it also left the battlefield littered with a large quantity of unexploded 8" artillery shells.*)

13th Wet again & very cold. Heard that the Russians are advancing, & driving back the Austrians very successfully. At 4 p.m. called out along with 3 other lorries to proceed to battery to fetch back the ammunition which we took up the preceeding (*preceding*) night. A very cold night. Saw a Bantam Battalion. (*Bantam Infantry Battalions were made up of strong and healthy soldiers who didn't quite match up to the minimum army recruitment height of 5ft 3 inches.*) Arrived back at 10 p.m.

14th At 8.30 a.m. took back to railhead this ammunition. The new canteen opened. At 11 a.m. orders received to get ready to leave here & so packed up & prepared for a long journey. After bidding good bye to all friends residing here, left the village at 2 p.m. after being stationed here over 9 months. All the French people sorry to lose us. We proceeded to battery & loaded lorry with officers (*Officer's*) kits. At 8 p.m. caterpillars pulled guns out of action & left this place, followed by the column. No one knew in what direction we had to go & at 1 a.m. halted by the road-side at a village called Dieval.

15th Got to bed & arose about 9 a.m. & prepared lorry for next journey. Had a walk round the village. This is a very pretty part. At 8 p.m. the column left here followed by the guns & proceeded through St Pol, which is a very nice town, lying in a beautiful valley & halted for a rest etc at a village called Bouquemaison. After supper got to bed for a good rest. Arose at 9 a.m. Prepared lorry for following journey & had a walk round the place which is a few miles south of Fervent. Advanced clocks an hour.

16th Saw the J.C.S. (*Joint Chiefs of Staff*) column past & met with John & Ernie. Several batteries on the road travelling in the same direction as us. At 8 p.m. left here & travelled 18 mls (*miles*) or so, & halted at a village called Villers Bocage for the night. (*Not the famous World War Two battle ground in Normandy, this Villers-Bocage is a small village just a few miles north of Amiens.*) A nice place. The country is very pretty & there are exceptionally good roads in this district, the Somme. A hot day.

17th Had a few hours sleep & then busy with lorry for next journey. Left here at 9 p.m. & continued journey south through Amiens. This is a very nice town & is beautifully situated in a lovely valley. In this part the roadways have rows of apple-trees etc growing at the sides. A very cold night & arrived at our destination about 12 midnight. This is an S.A.P. & many lorries are stationed in this village, LaHoussaye (*La Houssaye*) (3rd Corps) attached to the guns & caterpillars arrived in the early morning.

18th Usual work on lorry. Got to know that about 100 lorries are stationed here for a short period, during the coming great offensive & over a 1000 A.S.C. men. A flying ground (*I think Frank is referring to an RFC airfield*) close at hand & very interesting to see the aeroplanes going out on there (*their*) splendid work.

At 8 p.m. the column set off to the position where the guns are to be in action, followed by the guns. This is at the town of Albert, a very pretty town in a beautiful valley. The Germans have occupied it 3 times. Arrived back at 1 a.m. Great sheets were nailed to trees along the road to this line to screen transports from being observed by the enemy. (*The most famous evidence of this type of camouflage can be seen on You Tube under the heading Hell-Fire Corner.*)

19th Another heavy battery of 8" guns arrived here during the night. Busy with lorries. Sir Douglas Haig's birthday (55). The workshop attached to 19th Siege arrived at Park. Aeroplanes very busy in this district. A pretty part, but drinking water is scarce, we have to walk a good distance to get it. We are stood on a main road, & it is surprising the amount of motor transports that pass.

20th Called up at 5 a.m. to proceed to rail-head for ammunition to a place called Dornarcourt (*Probably Dernancourt*). Loaded with 8" shells & returned to Albert & back to Park. Coming back the Germans shelled the road, but we got back safely. Attended to lorry. At 6 p.m. an aeroplane, on going up, suddenly broke down & alighted in a cornfield. Left the Park at 9 p.m., after just getting to bed & took it to Albert, returning at 1 a.m.

21st At 10 a.m. proceeded with 11 other lorries to railhead (Contay) for ammunition & returned to column without drawing any. Went again at 2 p.m. & arrived back at 7 p.m. Left for battery at 9 p.m. & returned 12.30 p.m. A splendid day. Aeroplanes very active. Major Moberly, awarded D.S.O. (**Distinguished Service Order**) & 2 gunners the D.C.M. (**Distinguished Conduct Medal**) for good work at the Loos Battle.

22nd Aeroplanes very active. Counted 18 Observation Balloons over our front observing, as a most favourable day for this work. Paid 20 francs. Busy cleaning lorry. Germans shelled one of the above mentioned balloons, but without success. The Russians still advancing. Given 18 gals (**gallons**) petrol for emergency.

23rd Usual work etc for day. A machinegun Corps (motorcyclist) passed here & several cavalry units. Also the following infantry regiments, 11 Border (Salford) Lancashire Fusiliers & the K.O.Y.L.I. (**Kings Own Yorkshire Light Infantry**)

24th A cold, wet day for June. Took lorry into workshop to have near side back spring repaired. Heavy thunderstorm & directly afterwards an intense bombardment for about ¼ hour. During the evening heavy firing along the front. Aeroplanes very active. Issued with a pair of trousers.

25th A fine day & much work observing done by our airmen. Half holiday given. At 9 p.m. called out to proceed to Contay for shell. 7 lorries went to above railhead & several took up ammunition. Arrived back at 12.30 p.m. A violent bombardment along this front.

26th Several showers. 14 observation balloons up. Still heavy firing by our guns. Busy on lorries. The Germans sent over several shells in this district. 2

of our caterpillars moved from the park, nearer to the guns in case we advanced.

27th Removed from the main Albert, Amiens road at La Houssoye (*Lahoussoye*), to village (Franvilliers) (*Franvillers*) about 2 kilometers (*kilometres*) away, as we were taking up too much of the road. Busy all day, & very showery. At 2 p.m. proceeded to guns with ammunition & arrived back at 5 p.m. Guns in action whilst there, & several batteries likewise. Heard that we gassed the Germans 3 times during the morning. At 9 p.m. went to railhead (Contay) for shell, & arrived back at 2.30 a.m.

28th Very wet morning. Heavy bombardment along the whole British front. Several lorries took up ammunition & several went to load up. British gun fire brought down 3 German observation balloons & heard that we had broken the German front line in 10 different places.

29th Busy on lorries. At 11.30 a.m. took up ammunition to battery & arrived back at 3 p.m. Coming home No. 5 lorry broke down & we towed it home to the column. The head of piston completely broken out of front cylinder. Our guns firing heavily on this front. Aeroplanes, & observation balloons very actively engaged observing.

30th At 8 a.m. proceeded to Contay for ammunition & arrived back at 11.30 a.m. Burst petrol pipe returning. A splendid day. Terrific bombardment along the whole British front. Our Navy given a free hand & the Declaration of London quashed. (*The declaration of London concerned Britain's Laws governing its Naval Warfare and wartime activities, by quashing this declaration the Royal Navy were being given a looser rein when planning their campaigns.*) The Tyneside battalions billeted here, went into action tonight, & the 7th Suffolks came into the village. All loaded lorries took there (*their*) ammunition to battery.

1st July 1916 A splendid day & heavy bombardment of the enemy's lines by our artillery. Issued with a new respirator & given a road map. Official news that the British attack most successful & that we had agained (*gained*) all objectives & took 4 lines of trenches. Many wounded coming back, many who went up last night. German aeroplanes brought down & the captives taken prisoners. They came past here. The Suffolks move off & the Durham Light Infantry came in & took over their billets. (*Battle of the Somme. 1 July 1916 – 18 November 1916. Authors note: This was the first day of the Battle of the Somme and I expected some sort of monumental description in the diary about what Frank did on this historic day. The reality for Frank was that it was just another battle on just another day. On the first day of the battle the British Army famously suffered nearly 58,000 casualties of which about 19,000 died, by 18 November 1916 the total number of British, French and German soldiers that had been killed was staggering, it is believed to be the costliest battle of the First World War. In five senseless months of attrition the British Army had advanced only 6 miles on a 16 mile front, and its only other accomplishment was to take some pressure off the French troops fighting down at Verdun. A little known fact is that the Army Service Corps lorry's returning from the battery after unloading their ammunition, helped to transport casualties back towards the nearest Field Ambulance or Casualty Clearing Station.*)

2nd At 9 a.m. all loaded lorries took ammunition to the guns. We arrived back at 12.30 a.m. & proceeded to Pontvillers for another load. Arrived back at 8.30 p.m. & at 9.30 p.m. took same to battery & arrived back at 2.30 a.m. 1st time I had taken 2 loads in 1 day to guns. Whilst at Pontvillers saw a train load of German prisoners (640). All were well clothed & looked well. Terrific bombardment by our artillery & heard that all was going well in the great attack. Aeroplanes very active. The Durham's (*Durham Light Infantry*) went into action.

3rd Busy working on lorries. Many men with slight wounds came to the rest-stations here & several lorries in the park claimed to fetch back the wounded. 3 German prisoners passed here under an escort. Heavy artillery engagement by our guns.

4th Usual work for day. Several lorries took up ammunition & fetched back wounded. A terrible thunderstorm passed over during the afternoon. On guard for the 23rd time. At 1 a.m. lorry's empty proceeded to Pushvillers (*Puchevillers*) for ammunition & arrived back at 5.30 a.m. The Germans counter-attacked heavily to the left of Albert during the night, & our guns replied tremendously. A most terrific bombardment, which was most successful. Heard that the great offensive was still progressing favourably.

5th Prepared lorry for next journey. Aeroplanes very active. Heavy bombardment during the morning. The heavy rains suspended operations for a time. The Welsh Regiment left here for the front & the Gordon Highlanders came in. (*These Regiments were all part of 76th Brigade commanded by Major Generals J.A. Haldane and C.J. Deverell.*) Took ammunition (7 lorries) to the battery & returned at 11 p.m. 50 lorries in park went to Pushvillers & loaded with ammunition for the French.

6th Fine day & much observing by aircraft. The British still bombarding the enemy's lines heavily. The Gordon's (*Gordon Highlanders Infantry Regiment*) left here for the front. The following troops passed here on their way up, The Kings Own, 2nd Suffolks, & the Fusiliers. At 11 p.m. left here for Pushvillers (*Puchevillers*) for ammunition. 12 lorries went & all got back to column at 7 a.m. next morning.

7th Had breakfast & got lorry ready for the next journey & then went to bed for the rest of the day. Paid 20 francs. At 7.30 p.m. left here for battery, & returned at 11.30 p.m. A very wet afternoon & night. All going well in the advance. Many wounded coming back, a good percentage only slight wounds though.

8th Busy on lorries. A hot day after yesterday's heavy rains. The Munster Fusiliers came into this village. The Russians still capturing many prisoners & advancing strongly. Heavy bombardment along this front & aeroplanes very busy.

9th A splendid day. At 7.15 a.m. proceeded to Contay with 14 other lorries for shell. Reached column at 11.30 a.m. & in the afternoon several lorries took up the ammunition to battery. The Germans hit a bomb store above Albert in our lines & it exploded. A terrific bombardment on this front from 8 p.m. & continued through the night.

10th Another fine day & all going well at the front. Several lorries went to Dornercourt (**Probably Dernancourt**) for ammunition, but returned empty. Sir Douglas Haig passed here. Saw the 1st ambulance fitted with steel screen as a protection from shrapnel. Our guns firing heavy at Albert & district. Proceeded to battery with 11 other lorries with ammunition at 8 p.m. & arrived back at 1 a.m. Battery in action while there.

11th Damaged radiator on No 7 lorry, damaged estimated at £1. (**£92.76p in today's valuation.**) Both my mate & myself put under arrest. At 11 a.m. proceeded to Contay with empties & returned at 1 p.m. Going we were stopped by the police for using a wrong road. Saw 8 German prisoners, 2 German officers, & 2 field guns pass here. At 8.30 p.m. proceeded to Contay for ammunition and returned at 1 a.m. Terrific bombardment all night.

12th At 9.30 a.m. we both appeared before the major of the III Corps Siege Park & were tried. A fine sensation. Major J.G.L Flydell Nott, A.S.C. C.O. of Park tried us & deprived us both of 2 days' pay. (**This would have amounted to just over 2 Shillings each because the average soldiers pay in 1916 was a Shilling a day, a not inconsiderable amount of money to a lowly Private in the Army Service Corps. Still, the army would have to cover the outstanding 16 Shillings of the £1 needed to repair the radiator.**) Heard that our troops had taken Contalmaison. The West Yorks came in the village for the night, on their way back for a rest. Took ammunition to battery at 5.30 p.m. & returned with a load of empties at 8.30 p.m.

13th At 9 a.m. took empties to railhead & returned 12 noon. (**The British Army had started recycling as much material as they could because everything was**

in short supply, empty shell cases were returned to the UK to be smelted down and re-used.) The 2nd, 4th, & 5th Dragoon Guards, 11 Hussars, 9th Lancers, & signallers & Machine Gun Corps passed through here. 4 German prisoners also passed here. A Brigade of R.H.A. (*Royal Horse Artillery*) came through the village about 7 p.m.

14th A fine day & much observing being done by our aircraft. Heard that the Bengal Lancers had broken the German line on a 6000 yards front with great success. (*This probably refers to the Battles of Bazentin Ridge and Delville Wood, although the Lancers fought with great bravery any successes about them were greatly exaggerated.*) At 8 p.m. proceeded to Albert to help to move the 69th Battery R.G.A. (*Royal Garrison Artillery*) 8" Howitzers, but returned at 11 p.m., our services not being required. Several German guns captured.

15th A very hot day. At 10 a.m. proceeded to Dornarcourt (*Probably Dernancourt*) for ammunition, & returned to column at 1 .30 p.m. Noticed that all caterpillars from III Corps Siege Park were moving up towards Albert to be nearer the guns. Several lorries went to Contay for ammunition. Saw about 100 German prisoners. Our guns firing heavy. Up to date our guns have each fired 5,000 rounds whilst in France, & said to be in excellent condition yet. The K.O.S.B. (*Kings Own Scottish Borderers*) came into billets here, before going into action.

16th At 9 a.m. proceeded to Albert with ammunition & returned at 12 noon. 170 rounds taken up. At 6 p.m. proceeded to Dornarcourt (*Probably Dernancourt*) for ammunition & took it to battery & returned to column at 10.30 p.m. A very wet night. Many wounded returning.

17th At 6.30 a.m. proceeded to Dernancourt along with 5 other lorries to do work for the Royal Engineers. A foggy day & the Germans took advantage of it & counter-attacked on several fronts of the line. A very wet afternoon. Returned to column at 6.30 p.m.

18th Called out at 5 a.m. to work for the Royal Engineers. Saw a 12 inch naval gun (armoured train) fire, for the 1st time. Also a 15" howitzer, on the return journey to column. Several heavy batteries advancing on this front. Was at the 1st line of German trenches held by them (before the advance). Had a good look round.

19th On engineers work again, loading stone from Albert station to the R.E.'s. A section of the 37th Royal Fusiliers, Labour Battalion assisted us. During the dinner hour the Germans sent over about 20 shells, all dropping in the town of Albert. All took cover for a time. Returned to column at 7 p.m. During the night No's 1 & 2 guns of our battery advanced; taking up a new position near Mametz, east of Fricourt.

20th A very hot day. Many troops being moved. No 3 & 4 guns moved to the above position at Mametz. At 2 p.m. proceeded to the battery along with 11 other lorries to move all stores etc. Saw many interesting things during the afternoon for here, the Germans were, not a month ago. The villages of Fricourt & Mametz are shelled to the ground. Arrived back at 8 p.m.

21st Busy on lorry all day. On guard at night for the 24th time. Paid 20 francs. Several Taubes ventured over our lines in the Albert district & heard that 2 had been brought down. At 12 midnight several lorries went to Contay for ammunition & several lorries took up ammunition to new position. The 10th Northumberland Fusiliers came in here for a rest.

22nd Usual work. A sergent (*Sergeant*) from the base posted to our section. A 3 pounder, quick firing gun was dug out of an old German trench by the gunners of our battery. A 15" shell from one of our guns in the bombardment had buried it. It was ready to fire & is in good condition, bar a wheel which has 3 spokes knocked out. Terrific bombardment by our guns commenced at 11 p.m. All going well for us on this front.

23rd Called up at 5 a.m. & proceeded to battery with 7 other lorries with ammunition & arrived back at 10 a.m. Many wounded being brought back after the attack of the last night. Heavy bombardment by all the guns on this front during the night. Our troops fighting in Pozieres & heard that the French had captured Piroone (*Peronne*).

24th Proceeded to Albert to the battery's old position along with 10 other lorries & moved all ammunition from there to the new position. Each took up 2 loads. Returned at 4 p.m. Many cavalry troops passed through here. The Germans counterattacked 3 times & were repulsed each time by the Australian Divisions with heavy losses. While we were at the battery & coming through Albert the Germans sent over several shells, some dropping quite close. At 8 p.m. proceeded to Meaulte for ammunition, returning at 3 a.m.

25th All going well on this front. The British still bombarding the German lines immensely. Aeroplanes very active & several squadrons crossed over here at a great height, as if carrying out a raid.

26th Severe fighting taking place on this front & many wounded being brought back. Splendid work done by the Australian Divisions. (*Although the battle of Pozieres (23 July – 3 September 1916) included both British and Australian Divisions, it is today primarily famous for being an Australian victory. 1 ANZAC Corps suffered over 25,000 casualties.*) The Northampton's came in here for a rest. At 8.30 a.m. paraded with rifle & smoke helmets & an inspection by Lieu (*Lieutenant*) Young. Strict orders that no lights or smoking to be allowed in ammunition lorries.

27th A splendid day & very hot. Busy cleaning lorry. Terrific bombardment by the British on this front. Aeroplanes very active & all going well.

28th Usual work for day. Heard of great Russian success. Still bombarding the enemy's lines & the Germans returned the fire very heavily at intervals. 2

gunners of the battery caught 2 spies in Fricourt, dressed thus, German trousers & French tunics.

29th A very hot day. A few Taubes ventured over our lines but soon were driven back. Zeppelin raid on the East Coast again. (***This was a ten Zeppelin raid that achieved very little because nearly half of them turned back because of mechanical problems.***) Heavy bombardment by the British. Nothing unusual to note.

30th Terribly hot day. Several lorries took ammunition to the battery & whilst there several shells came over quite close to the guns& so everyone took cover. The Northampton's moved up the line & the E. (***East***) Lancashire's came in to the village for a rest.

31st At 8 a.m. took up ammunition to battery, along with 7 other lorries & arrived back at 12 noon. While there the Germans shelled this part a lot & we had a narrow escape. Saw one drop amongst a lot of horses & it did much damage. At 2 p.m. 5 Taubes were over Franvillers & our machines gave chase & we heard afterwards that 2 had been brought down.

1st August 1916 A very hot day & aeroplanes very actively engaged. All going well at the front & the British still keeping up a heavy bombardment. Busy on lorries etc. Several German prisoners repairing the roads in this part. (***Under modern rules of the Geneva Convention this wouldn't be allowed to happen, all Prisoners of War must be removed to a safe area after being captured and cannot be used to enhance an enemy's fighting capabilities, albeit repairing roads.***)

2nd Several lorries loaded up with shell & 5 took same to battery. The Germans shelled Albert very heavily & also our lines & in the evening they counterattacked but without success. A very hot day again.

3nd Usual work for day. The Highland Light Infantry came here for a rest. Albert again shelled & a lorry belonging this park whilst passing through with 24 gunners, who were coming back for a rest, was hit, both drivers & 3 gunners killed & the remainder all wounded. The lorry badly damaged. On guard for the 25th time. Paid 20 francs.

4th We fetched the rations & water for day. Again very hot. Several of the men of the column went for a swim & we all enjoyed it. Still heavy firing by our guns & much ammunition being used & the troops still holding all ground.

5th Took over a 5 ton lorry & for the present it is fetching rations & water for the park daily. (*This 5 ton lorry could be either a Leyland or Daimler because most military lorry's were of a 3 ton weight.*) Very hot indeed. Several Taubes ventured over our lines, but were driven back. During the night there was a most terrific bombardment by our guns.

6th Heard of more zeppelin raids over England & of the awful murder of Capt Fryatt. (*Captain Charles Algernon Fryatt was a Merchant Navy Mariner who had been challenged several times by German U-Boats whilst crossing between the continent and England. On several occasions he defied German orders to heave-to and he even tried to ram the submarines to avoid being boarded, searched and then sunk by them. The British nation showed their appreciation of his belligerence and courage by awarding him a couple of inscribed pocket watches that commemorated his heroism. On his last crossing Charles was the Captain of S.S. (Steam-Ship) Brussels and he was captured just off the coast of the Netherlands by a German U-Boat and they found the inscribed watches on his person. The Germans arranged a Court Martial in Bruges and Charles was found guilty and sentenced to death for illegally attacking German submarines and on 27 July 1916 sentence was carried out by a German firing squad.*) Heard officially of more Russian successes & also a great Italian offensive taking place. Usual work for day & again very hot.

7th Bank Holiday but no holiday for us. Our aeroplanes very active, & several Taubes driven to earth, more or less damaged. Several lorries took up ammunition & some drawn from dump at LaHoussaye. About 40 men from battery sent back for a rest. Heard that Capt (*Captain*) Campbell of the 19th Siege had died of wounds in England, caused by the blowing up of an ammunition dump near his battery, by the Germans.

8th Heavy bombardment on this front by the British & several lorries took up ammunition. Others on Royal Engineers work. Very hot day. Issued with a new mess-can. The Germans still attacking at Verdun against the French but without success.

9th Nothing of great importance happening on this front, all being very quiet at present. The Germans sent over a few shells into Albert. Our aeroplanes very active. The 6th East Yorks came in here for a rest. More from battery came back from a rest in the village & the others returned.

10th Good news to hand of the Russian offensive & that the French were attacking the Bulgarians at Salonicka (*Salonica*). The big offensive now being carried out on all the fronts. Heavy bombardment on this front during the evening. Heard that one of our captive balloons had broken loose & sailed over the German lines.

11th Very hot during the afternoon, but a nice shower in the early morning. Our troops still gaining ground around Pozieres. 10 lorry load of ammunition taken up at night & several lorries loaded up at railhead at Contay.

12th During the day Albert was again heavily shelled & I noticed that the house, where the officers of our battery billeted, when in the Albert position, had been struck by a shell & half the house demolished. Heard that 3 Staff officers were in the house at the time & that all were killed. Very hot during the day. Seven lorries (*This is the first time in the diary that Frank has used a* *written numerical word for the amount of vehicles used.*) took up ammunition during the evening. On guard for the 26th time.

13th Very hot again. 6 lorries took up ammunition & several went to draw at railhead. Official news that the great Austrian town of Gorizia had fallen into the hands of the Italians, who are carrying out a most vigorous offensive, most successfully & that the Russians are pressing on Lemberg in the east. (*6th-17th August 1916 was the sixth Battle of Gorizia, or as it is more commonly known, Isonzo. Eventually there were twelve battles of Isonzo between the Italians and Austro-Hungarians and although the Italians are credited with winning this battle, the casualty figures portray a much sadder story. The Austro-Hungarian soldiers were the better equipped and trained soldiers and to compensate for this the Italians threw a wall of soldiers against them which resulted in them suffering considerably more casualties. Gorizia remains a part of Italy.*)

14th Very showery & much cooler. The British gained more ground west of Poziers & the French have gained ground too near Peroone (*Peronne*). While sat having tea, heard screams of fire & found out a farm yard & buildings had caught fire. All lorries were moved from the danger zone & all drivers brought their extinguishers (about 120 in all) & played on it, but to no advantage. By 6 oclock it was completely gutted. A most startling adventure. The King on a visit to the front in France, has inspected troops & captured positions on the Somme (this front). (*This entry didn't make much sense to me until I read it again just before publishing the book. The King inspected the troops before having a look around some captured German positions seized during the Battle of the Somme. The King himself obviously wouldn't have captured positions during the battle of the Somme.*)

15th Very showery all day. Heavy bombardment by the British on this front. Several lorries on Engineers work & 6 went to Contay for ammunition. Saw an aeroplane land at this aerodrome & on landing the propeller & engine buried themselves in the ground & much damage done to the machine. Pilot injured.

16th Usual work for day. Heavy bombardment by the British & Germans shelled the vicinity of Albert, Fricourt & Contalmaison very heavily. At 10 p.m. 10 lorries called out to take ammunition to the guns & returned at 2 a.m. A very hot day. 30 of our aeroplanes counted over the German lines on this front, at 8 a.m.

17th Very showery & very much dirt again & roads in bad condition, like winter. Noticed several of our aeroplanes going over the German lines, at a great height, and most likely carrying out a raid. The 10th Lincolns came in here for a rest. (***This is the first and only time in the diary that Frank has used the word 'and' instead of using the ampersand symbol.***)

18th A hot day. Paid 20 francs. Aeroplanes very busy & a beautiful day for observation. Issued with a new fire extinguisher. The British still keeping up a heavy bombardment of the enemie's (***enemy's***) lines & heard that the advance was still continuing.

19th A very wet day. Usual work. The Lincoln's left here. Several lorries on Engineer's work & 7 took up ammunition & 5 loaded with same at dump. A fire piquet formed on each column & drills & practice to be done regarding same, in case of fire. Many German's (prisoners) repairing the main Albert-Amiens road. All look happy & same glad to be prisoners of war.

20th A splendid day. Cricket match in the afternoon between the 39th A.S.C. & the 19th. The 39th won by 4 runs. A good game all through. Several men of the column permitted to go for a swim in the river. 5 load of ammunition taken to battery. Several Taubes over the British lines & 2 were brought down.

21st Very hot day. A new 6" howitzer battery joined the strength of the park. All Derby men. 2 men from the base posted to our column. The Germans shelled Albert & Fricourt very freely. Our troops still doing well on this front.

22nd An 8" howitzer battery joined this park. The A.S.C. men attached to same, said to be conscripts. (***Conscription for the British Army started on 2nd March 1916, so these Army Service Corps drivers could well have been Conscripted Soldiers.***) Saw another aeroplane, badly damaged on landing at aerodrome. A terrific bombardment by the British & several lorries took up ammunition.

23rd The 47th Division came down to this part. The Post Office Rifles (London Regiment) are billeted here. On guard for the 27th time, & very busy presenting arms etc to the staff of this Division. All going well with the Allies on all fronts. Heard that the Nottingham & Falmouth had been sunk by a German submarine. (***HMS Nottingham was a British Light Cruiser that was sunk by three torpedoes from U-52 on 19th August 1916, 38 sailors died***

during the attack and the ship sank just off Flamborough Head on the East Yorkshire coast. HMS Falmouth was a similar class of ship and she was sunk during the same action by attacks from submarines U-63 and U-66, she also lies just off Flamborough Head.)

24th One of the guns of our battery moved to a new position at Contalmaison. A very warm spot. Usual work for day. Great success by the French who have taken Maurepas, (***French part of the Battle of the Somme.***) & a good day for the British. Several lorries took up ammunition to battery. The Germans shelling the road in Albert, 3 kilometres this side (*of*) the town.

25th A splendid day & aeroplanes very busy. Counted 16 battle-planes going over the German lines at a great altitude & most likely carrying out a raid. Heard bombardment by the British & French on this front. 2 old Thornycroft lorries sent to the base being unfit for further use in an ammunition column.

26th Very showery all day. Saw the transports of the Guards Division came through here & heard that the troops were moving up by rail. They are to take part in the offensive on this front. 8 lorries took up ammunition, 2 going to the gun at Contalmaison. This gun only fired 6 rounds so far it being near the enemy lines.

27th A very wet day. 8 lorries took up ammunition to the battery. Several lorries on Engineers work. During the evening, whilst fine & clear, many of our aeroplanes up. The left half gunners of our battery came out for their 1st rest after 15 months in action & were relieved by men of the 135th battery.

28th Another wet day. Official news that Italy had declared war on Germany, & Romania had declared war on Austria. (***Both of these declarations actually happened on the 27th August 1916.)*** Operations on this front sorely impeded by the heavy rains of the last few days. Counted 16 aeroplanes going in the direction of the German lines & no doubt carrying out a raid.

29th A fearful wet day, & a terrific thunderstorm here during the afternoon. Many transports on their way to the front. 2 lorries took up ammunition to No 4 gun at Contalmaison. Commenced to parade at 8.30 p.m. (Roll call)

30th Still heavy rains & roads in a fearful state. Operations stopped on the front & all quiet, bar slight artillery duels. Too bad weather for our aeroplanes to go up.

31st Several lorries carting stones for the Engineers. At 8 p.m. 7 lorries took up ammunition to the battery, returning at 1 a.m. The Germans shelled our lines very heavily at intervals. Nothing important to note today.

1st September 1916 A fine day & drying up a lot. Terrific bombardment by our guns during the evening. 4 lorries took up shell to the battery & several drew ammunition at the railhead. Aeroplanes very active. Paid 20 francs. Heard of great riots at Salonika by the Greeks. (*King Constantine of Greece wanted his country to remain neutral during World War 1 but other Greek political bodies remained sympathetic to the allied cause. This animosity led to rioting on the streets of Salonika which resulted in the deaths of 82 Greek and 194 Allied soldiers.*)

2nd Another fine day. The British still carrying out the offensive on this front & heard that all was going in our favour. On guard at night for the 28th time.

3rd Usual work for day. Lorries very busy taking up ammunition to battery & loading again at railhead. Fine clear day & aeroplanes very busy & 3 Taubes brought down. Heavy bombardment took place during the night.

4th A wet day. Sir Douglas Haig passed through this village. The Rumanians advanced about 25 miles into Hungry. Zeppelin raid on England, one being brought down. 4 lorries took up shell to battery.

5th Good news from the front & the French doing splendidly. The town of fell into the hands of the Rumanians & the Russians reported captured another20,000 prisoners. Heavy bombardment along this front. About 6000 Germans taken prisoner by the French on this front & capture of 31 guns.

6th A fine day & many aeroplanes up. Heavy bombardment on this front, the heaviest known & the Germans said to be preparing a treat. Several batteries of field artillery came out of action for a rest. The right half of 19th Siege came out for a rest.

7th A busy day & much ammunition taken from this park to respective batteries. Saw an aeroplane meet with an accident on leaving the ground. Badly damaged but pilot not hurt. 4 German machines brought down, 3 falling in our lines & the other came down in no-mans-land, our artillery opening fire on it & destroyed it.

8th Many New Zealand troops passed here. All were fine, healthy men. Terrific bombardment on this front during the evening & heard of a success by the French. Major Noberly, promoted to Lieu-Colonel & the battery is now in charge of Major   (*As you can see from the diary entry below, Frank didn't actually write the name of the new Officer Commanding.*)

8th Many New Zealand troops passed here. All were fine, healthly men. Terrific bombardment on this front during the evening. & heard of a success by the French. Major Moberly, promoted to Lieu-Colonel & the battery is now in charge of Major

9th Took the 5 ton Halley (*Like the Albion Motor Company, Halley was another Glasgow based Motor Vehicle Company that produced both vehicles and artillery shells during the Great War.*) to Headquarters & brought back a 4 ton Saurer, 37 H.P. & took over charge of the same. A very hot day & many aeroplanes above. Several lorries took ammunition to the battery & another gun moved from Mametz to Contalmaison. (*Saurer was a Motor Company that was based in Sweden, the above mentioned 37 H.P. lorry had a 5 Litre 4 cylinder engine. Unlike the Thornycroft, the Saurer was driven by four wheels on the rear axle instead of the usual two, this lorry was considered to be a bit of a beast by some army drivers.*)

N.F. Clay

SAURER LORRY

10th Commenced to thoroughly clean etc the Saurer. At 2.30 p.m. church parade. 9 lorries went to load with ammunition & took same to battery. Went with J. Shaw on No 4 lorry to load with shells at Dernarcourt (***Dernancourt***) & arrived back at 2 a.m. on the 11th. Our batteries firing heavy through the night.

11th Usual work for day. The Post Office Rifles left here for the front as part of the 47th Division. (***The Post Office Rifles were formed in 1868 as a Volunteer unit and it eventually became part of the Territorial Army. On 20th September 1917 Sergeant Alfred Knight was a 29 year old platoon Sergeant serving in 2/8th (City of London) Battalion, London Regiment (Post Office Rifles) when his Platoon came under heavy machine-gun fire at Hubner Farm near Ypres . He rushed through an allied barrage and captured the enemy gun single handed. He performed several other acts of conspicuous bravery, all under heavy machine-gun and rifle fire and without regard to personal safety. When all the platoon officers had become casualties, he took***

command not only of his own platoon but of all the other platoons without officers. His energy in consolidating and reorganising was untiring. He died on 4 December 1960. Sergeant Alfred Knight is the only member of this unique organisation to win the Victoria Cross.) The 1st Division coming out of action. 6 lorries took up ammunition & 4 on Engineers work. 11 motor charabans (*charabancs*) passed here loaded with German prisoners.

12th Every available lorry went to load up & at night took ammunition to the battery. All very busy. Heard that the British & French were still advancing successfully on this front.

13th Usual work for day. Very showery. 2 Taubes over here, but were quickly driven back over their own lines. 8 lorries left park at 10 p.m. & proceeded to Dernarcourt for ammunition & took some on to battery arriving back at 6 a.m. on the 14th.

14th A nice day, but very cold at night. On guard for the 29th time. Very heavy bombardment to the left of Albert during the night & during the day the Germans shelled Albert, but did no great damage.

15th Half-holiday given & all had a game at cricket. 4 lorries loaded with ammunition at dump. At 6 p.m. 7 lorries proceeded to Vivviers mill Railhead & loaded with shell, & then took same to battery at Contalmaison. 1st time out with the Saurer. Great attack by British on this front & 1st time used the new armoured caterpillars. They are a great success. Our troops doing splendid work & Martinpuich (*Situated 18 miles south of Arras.*) has been captured. Arrived back at 2 a.m.

16th Paid 20 francs. Very wet during the morning. All heavy batteries on this front are moving up & the traffic on the road is enormous. Prepared lorry for next journey. The 1st Division called back to the trenches & the 1st Gloucesters left here. (*Gloucester Infantry Regiment who were often referred to as the 'Glorious Glosters.*)

17th At 10 a.m. left column with 4 other lorries & proceeded to Mametz & moved all gun-stores & ammunition up to the new position at Contalmaison. This made 3 trips to there & it is a very warm spot, the Germans shell it regularly. Our battery in action. Saw a Lieu Colonel (**Lieutenant Colonel**) of the German Army & his batman being brought in as prisoners. The former was wearing the crow cross (**Probably an Iron Cross medal for gallantry.**) Saw the new armoured caterpillars in Contalmaison. Many prisoners coming in.

18th At 7.30 a.m. proceeded to Mametz again to carry out the same work. Brought back a load of empty cartridge-cases. A fearfully wet day. 12 lorries took up ammunition to Contalmaison & the roads being so bad, it was an awkward job. No 1 Thornycroft got ditched & even a caterpillar could not move it, when the load was taken off.

19th A very wet day, & nothing of any account happened. The 7th Camerons came in to billets here for a rest. 10 lorries took up ammunition to the battery.

20th Still raining & operations severely checked on this front. Several lorries carting stones for the Engineers, who are busy making the roads good over the captured ground. Heavy bombardment by our guns.

21st A fine day. Took a load of empty cartridge cases to Contay railhead. 8 lorries took up ammunition to battery.

22nd Usual work for day. 10 lorries took up ammunition to the battery. A heavy bombardment by the British & a good many prisoners taken. The Germans shelled Albert.

23rd A fine day & usual cleaning of lorries & inspection of same. Aeroplanes very busy. Noticed battle-planes flying in the direction of the German lines at a great height & no doubt carrying out a raid. Saw an aviator on descending at aerodrome at LaHousagge loop the loop four times.

24th A fine, hot day. Was Regimental Policeman for day. 3 Derby men attached to the column. A heavy bombardment during the evening. At 8 p.m. proceeded to Dernancourt along with 9 other lorries to load with shell & returned to column at 12 midnight.

25th Usual work. At 10 a.m. proceeded to Contalmaison (10 lorries) with the ammunition. The Germans shelled the district very heavily & our guns were replying very sharply. Arrived back at 4.30 p.m. On guard for the 30th time. About 9.30 p.m. aircraft was over the French lines. The search-lights searching the sky & were a fine sight. We just caught sight of the machine which looked like a zeppelin.

26th Prepared lorry for next journey. At 2 p.m. proceeded to La Houssaye dump (10 lorries) & loaded up with ammunition & went straight up to Contalmaison returning to column at 8 p.m. Our guns firing heavily on this front & few German shelled (*shells*) came over but did no damage. 5 Taubes over Franvillers district.

27th Busy on lorry. At 11 a.m. proceeded to Dernancourt (10 lorries) & loaded with shell. Went to Contalmaison & delivered same to battery. Counted 28 of our aeroplanes over our front in the Contalmaison district. Returned to column at 4.30 p.m. Saw Earnie (***Ernie***). Paraded at 6.30 p.m. & our commanding officer told us that men of the 19 th Siege Ammunition Column had been awarded the Military Medal for good work & devotion to duty. This includes all of us. It was drawn for, as to who should wear it & Pte F Ward was the lucky one. (***This could possibly have been a similar award to the French Croix de Guerre (Cross of War), these honours were often awarded to both individuals and units of foreign armies, who served alongside the French Forces and provided distinguished and gallant service.***)

28th A very busy day. Heard officially that 2 zeppelins had been brought down in England. A great day for the French & British, the French captured Combles & the British Thiepval. *(After taking the Thiepval ridge the following Battle of Ancre Heights began on 1st October 1916.)* The M. J. inspectors paid a visit to our column. Passed my lorry & found everything satisfactory & was altogether pleased with the condition of lorries. Pte G Lydenham was put on the lorry with me.

29th Usual work for day. Lorries on Engineers work. 5 lorries went to load & took up the ammunition to the battery. Very showery. Terrific bombardment by the Allies on this front. Many French (M.J.) lorries came down to this part & took back a division, that had just come out of action.

30th Usual work. At 6 p.m. proceeded to Vivviersmill (7 lorries) & loaded with ammunition & took it up to a position at High Wood beyond Bazentin-le-Petit. No 3 & 4 guns moved up to here during the evening. This is within 1 ½ miles of the front line & the warmest spot I have ever been in. Shells were bursting at close quarters to us all the time. In this place for 4 hrs on account of No 14 lorry getting ditches. *(Frank probably meant ditched but see below diary entry.)*

Our guns are in the same positions as field batteries are here. While at railhead, taube came over & dropped several bombs. Arrived back 5.30 a.m.

1st October 1916 Attended to lorry & had rest of day in bed. Clocks put back an hour. 5 lorries took up ammunition & was transferred to G.S. (*General Service*) waggons at Contalmaison, it being too dangerous to take up motor lorries. (*G S Waggons were horse drawn and they resembled the pioneer* *wagons used in cowboy films of the 1950's, minus the white tarpaulin cover and hooped superstructure of course.*) A new wheel taken to No 3 gun, it being badly damaged, as soon as it was pulled into position. Another zeppelin brought down in North London.

2nd At 7 a.m. proceeded to Pont Noyelles (4 lorries) & loaded with bushes, for road making for the Engineers & took same to Albert. A very wet day. Arrived back at 4 p.m. The British attacked successful (*successfully*) near Le Sars (*Located on the Bapaume to Albert road*). 7 lorries took up ammunition & until further notice, G S waggons are to take the shells up to High Wood it being too dangerous for lorries.

3rd At 7 a.m. proceeded to Albert to carry trees for the Engineers. Took loads to Poziers & returned to column at 4.30 p.m. 6 lorries took up ammunition.

4th A very wet day & nothing important occurred. A division coming out of action was conveyed to their destination by French motor-buses.

5th Another wet day. Usual work cleaning lorries. I took up ammunition & returned at 8.30 p.m. Roads very bad again.

6th Usual work. Several lorries on Engineers work. The 7th Camerons (*Queens Own Cameron Highlanders*) left here for the front. Aeroplanes very busy, in spite of a strong breeze blowing. The 4th East York's (Territorials) came in here to billets.

7th At 4 a.m. 7 lorries took up ammunition to the guns & returned at 10 a.m. A 3 days bombardment by our guns said to commence this morning. French transports busy moving British troops.

8th A very wet day. At 2 p.m. proceeded to rail-head (7 lorries) & loaded with ammunition & took it on to the battery at Contalmaison. Met 300 German prisoners being brought in. They had been captured during the morning & all looked in an awful state. Arrived back at 10 p.m. Roads very bad.

9th The 18th London Regiment (Irish) came in here from the trenches. The 47th Division coming out of action & said to be going back to Abbeville to be reformed & brought up to strength. Their band & pipes played in the village during the evening. All available lorries took up ammunition to battery (14 lorries). On guard for the 31st time. Enemy aircraft over this part during the night.

10th A fine day. Busy cleaning lorries. Heard of a great victory by the Italians. 6 lorries took up ammunition. 9 lorries of the column are at present broken down. 2 on Engineers work.

11th At 8.30 a.m. proceeded to railhead (7 lorries) & loaded with ammunition & took same to Contalmaison returning to Park at 2 p.m. Our airmen very active over the front lines. The Germans shelled the roads very heavily which we had to go by. Fetched the water & rations for column in the afternoon. An old worn-out Thornycroft left the column as unsuitable & was sent to the base.

12th Ration work in the morning. At 2 p.m. proceeded to railhead (9 lorries) & loaded with ammunition returning to the column at 4 p.m.   At 6 p.m. orders came for the same lorries to take it to the battery. During the time we were at battery the Germans attacked & every gun of the British & French on this front opened fire & it was soon over. Returned to column at 11 p.m.

13th Ration work in the afternoon. Attended to lorry during the morning. Heavy bombardment during the day. 2 French aeroplanes landed at the aerodrome here. Very fine machines. The Germans shelled Albert during the day.

14th Ration work for day. A very cold day. 11 lorries took up ammunition to the battery. 4 lorries on Engineers work.

15th Ration work as usual. All available lorries took up ammunition to battery. 7 lorries having to return to railhead & deliver to battery a 2nd load. Each gun said to have about 800 rounds each at present.

16th Took over Peerless 3184 & the Saurer was detailed for ration work for regular. A Thornycroft of the 37th Siege battery put on the strength of the column. Heavy bombardment by the French & British. New front springs & chain (driving) fitted to lorry. 8 lorries took up ammunition.

17th At 3 p.m. left the park & proceeded to Heilly loaded with canteen stores, & took same to the 9th Divisional Transport lines returning to Park at 10.30 p.m. Had a fine time with the Quartermaster. Saw many Japanese Troops on this front, being conveyed in French (M.J.) Vehicles up the line. A very wet night. Paid 20 francs. Issued with new boots.

(The Japanese Armed Forces were British Allies during the First World War and their Imperial Navy fought alongside the Royal Navy in the Mediterranean Sea whilst based in Malta, they also took part in British operations off the coasts of South Africa and China. The Japanese took nearly 5,000 German Prisoners of War in China and all were treated extremely well. The soldiers that Frank mentions in his diary could well have been Canadian-Japanese soldiers who had to fight a lot of Canadian prejudice before being given permission to join the Canadian Army. They fought with much bravery and distinction on the Western Front and after the war they were given Canadian citizenship and eventually allowed to vote on political elections.)

18th A very wet night & the same this morning. Noticed an interment camp (cage) being made in the fields near this village for prisoners of war. At 2 p.m. proceeded to railhead (5 lorries) & loaded with ammunition (20 rounds) "as the roads are so very bad now" & took it on to the guns at Contalmaison. (*I can't understand why Frank used these speech marks in this part of the diary but they are definitely there.*) Burst water joint on engine before I reached there. All arrived back at 9 p.m.

19th Another wet day. 5 lorries loaded with ammunition & took same to guns. A most terrific bombardment during the day & aeroplanes very active. A Taube was brought down near our forward gun position, the pilot & observer being killed. Given half-holiday to play football. Very cold & all water ordered to be emptied out of engines. From this date radiators to be emptied (nightly). (*In the event of severe cold weather conditions, a vehicle radiator, and even an engine block can be ruptured through expanding frozen water in an engines cooling system.*)

20th A very sharp frost during the night. A violent bombardment also. An enemy aeroplane passed over here during the night & dropped several bombs at Corbie. Orders that in the future all to parade in drill order at 8.30 a.m.

21st Up at 5 a.m. 4 lorries proceeded on Engineers work at Albert. Took 1 load of stone to the La Boiselle road each & then returned home. Heavy bombardment during the night & this morning. The British & French had further success on this front & more prisoners were taken. Sharp frost & it was a fine day. The 7th W. (*West*) Yorks & E. (*East*) Yorks came in here for the night.

22nd The above troops moved off this morning for the front. At 10 a.m. proceeded to the High Wood position (6 lorries. 120 rounds) loaded off lorries on the main road. One lorry got ditched & we towed it out. Very heavy firing by the British guns on this front. Arrived back at 6 p.m. 6 lorries took up ammunition to Contalmaison.

23rd Usual work cleaning lorries & the drill parade at 8.30 a.m. 6 lorries took up ammunition to the battery. A very wet night. Great success by the French at Verdun. (*Frank is probably referring to the news that the French had recaptured Douaumont from the Germans whilst taking 6000 prisoners and seizing at least 15 pieces of artillery.*)

24th At 4 a.m. got ready for Albert, to do Engineers work. A very wet day & all quite (*quiet*) on this front except the usual artillery fire. Several shells sent over, dropping near Albert. Returned to column at 4 p.m.

25th Again much rain. On guard at night, (32nd time). The 6th Warwicks came here for 1 night, being brought by French Transports. All quiet on this front & nothing important doing.

26th Raining again & all operations greatly impeded. 1 lorry & 10 men left the column for Albert to clear the iron foundry which was burnt down by the Germans when they occupied the town, & to make room for all the lorries of the park to stand there.

27th Another wet day. Paid 20 francs. Usual work cleaning lorries. 7 lorries took up ammunition. The 8.30 a.m. drill parade dispensed with. A violent bombardment for about 2 hrs on this front during the evening. Passed a column of Japanese Motor Transports. They were in charge of French men. None seemed to be good drivers & they seem to have many accidents daily on these busy roads.

28th A fine day. 7 lorries took up ammunition to the battery. All the lorries needing repairs left the park for the new position at Albert. Half-holiday given.

27th. Another wet day. Paid 20 francs. Usual work cleaning lorries. 7 lorries took up ammunition. The 8.30a.m. drill parade dispensed with. A violent bombardment for about 2 hrs on this front during the evening. Passed a column of Japanese Motor Transports. They were in charge of French men. None seemed to be good drivers & they seem to have many accidents daily on these busy roads.

29th At 5 a.m. 10 lorries proceeded to rail head & loaded with ammunition. While there Pte Bainton moved the lorry up a yard or so & lost his head, the consequence was his lorry ran into the one in front & pushed same into the next, & the next bumped into mine. All together 3 lorries had their radiators badly damaged. £3 of his pay stopped. On leaving the guns, a driving chain broke & I was towed to Albert.

30th Busy in the foundry clearing up the iron. Heavy rain during the afternoon. The rest of the column came from Franvilliers to here to stay permanently. At dinner time the Germans shelled the town. 75% of the shells did not burst. Several men were wounded.

31st Again busy clearing up the yard. A fine day. Several lorries on Engineers work. Took off offside rear wheel & sent same to tyre press to be re tyred.

1st November 1916 Another fine day. During the night a Taube was over & dropped several bombs in this vicinity. 9 lorries went to load up & returned to park with the ammunition. Issued with fur coats.

2nd Same lorries took up the ammunition at 9.30a.m. & returned 12 noon. Every man in park on fatigue, squaring the position up. Heavy bombardment & many troops passed here on their way to the trenches. Taubes tried to come over our lines but were soon driven back with our air craft batteries (*Anti-aircraft Batteries*) & aeroplanes.

3rd A lovely day. Issued with new jerseys. All busy cleaning lorries. The Germans sent about 20 shells into the town about dinner, killing & wounding a few of our troops.

4th At 8 a.m. Lieu (*Lieutenant*) Young, Serg (*Sergeant*) Lovelace & 6 men including myself were given passes to search for German guns which have been captured on this front, within the 3rd Corps area. We proceeded to Contalmaison & then on to Mametz Wood. There we found many rounds of ammunition 2, 8.2 howitzers (captured from the Russians on the eastern front) & a 4.2 howitzer. Returned to park at 6 p.m.

5th Today searched Bazentin-le-Petit Wood, & to the outskirts of Martinpuch (*Martinpuich*) & High Wood. Found a German 8" howitzer buried in a dug out (*dugout*) & many rounds of ammunition. The British guns were bombarding the enemy lines on this front most violently all day. The Butte of Warlencourt captured in the attack. Saw in the distance Bapaume & in the outskirts of the town could be seen firing the enemy's field batteries. (*The Butte de Warlencourt was a prehistoric burial ground situated on the south-eastern side of the Albert to Bapaume road, from the early days of the war the Germans had held this high ground that dominated the surrounding area. This hillock was heavily defended by hundreds of German soldier's protected by dug-outs, tunnels and barbed-wire. The British troops defending their lower positions were constantly battered by German machine-guns, mortars* *and very accurate artillery fire directed by Forward Artillery Officers who had direct communication with the guns located behind on the high ground. The British didn't actually captured the Butte but took over the ground after the German retirement to the Hindenburg line in February 1917. Whilst Frank was in the area a 24 year old Lieutenant Colonel Roland Bradford was to win the Victoria Cross whilst attacking the Butte de Warlencourt. Between them, Roland and his brothers, George, Thomas, and James were to win an astonishing amount of gallantry medals that amounted to, two Victoria Crosses, a Distinguished Service Order and a Military Cross. Roland was killed in action on 30th November 1917.)*

6th A lovely day & a heavy bombardment. Taubes very active & several combats in the air took place. Warlencourt recaptured by the Germans. The Germans shelled Albert, killing several soldiers in billets. A lovely moonlight night & Taubes over this part. They dropped many bombs & a French ammunition dump heard to have been blown up. Heard many explosions as if this had happened.

7th Another fine day & aeroplanes very active. A Taube was brought down this morning on the main Albert-Amiens Road & one of ours came down, the pilot being severely wounded. He brought down the Taube mentioned. 8 lorries took up ammunition. 4 new 8" howitzers arrived here for the 39th Siege. Albert again shelled.

8th Our search party found 3 more guns in Caterpillar Wood. A very wet day. Put up a large tent for a recreation tent for the winter & fixed up a fire-grate & made all very comfortable. Lieu (**Lieutenant**) Farmer placed a good number of books etc in for us. Many troops passed through on their way up to the trenches.

9th A nice day. Our search-party went over high Wood district & found 3 German field guns. The Howitzer we found on the 4th in Mametz Wood was brought down to our Headquarters. Several Taubes over our lines. On guard for the 33rd time (with bayonet.) About 9 p.m. an enemy airman flew over the town very low & turned his machine gun on troops in the street, killing & wounding about 6. Another came over at 11 p.m. & dropped 2 bombs.

10th About 5 a.m. our batteries commenced a violent bombardment, being carried out all day. Our aeroplanes very active. Our search party found another gun & much ammunition in dug-outs. Went to Contalmaison to bring them home. Paid 20 francs. Taubes over this evening dropping many bombs.

11th At 8 a.m. 11 lorries proceeded to railhead & took 330 rds (**rounds**) to battery. Roads very heavy. Told that about 50 bombs were dropped in the vicinity of the railhead, last night, but no damage done. Heavy bombardment by the British still continues. All batteries up the line have many rounds at their positions.

12th Several lorries on Engineers work. Busy moving machinery in the yard all day & no half-holiday given. A very wet night. Bombardment still going heavy. The Germans shelled Albert during the night.

13th Fitted rear wheel on lorry & chains also. A dull, cold day. Albert again shelled. Still a terrific bombardment by our guns continue. A fatigue party left the column to dig out the guns found. Taubes again over during the night & many bombs were dropped. Our airmen went out, most likely on a raid.

14th Several lorries took up ammunition. Contalmaison heavily shelled, also the Bapaume Road. At 10.10 a.m. the Germans commenced to shell Albert quite close to our lorries, so all flew down the dug outs for shelter. 10 came over & then they stopped for an hour & then 10 more dropped right in the park. 1 hit a Daimler of the 26th Siege setting fire to it. Other lorries standing near caught fire also. 1 shell fell in the cyclist's hut, burning out all the motor-cycles. Orders given for all lorries to leave at once & get on the Amiens road. This caused a rush & then the streets were lined with lorries & traffic held up. About 8 men were injured & 2 were killed. I had to leave my lorry as repairs were being carried out to the steering. A shell dropped quite close to this lorry

& a great lump of iron fell into the beds. The Workshops returned to La Houssaye & the 19th, 39th, 40th, & 61st parked up along the roadside at Baizieux (*A few miles to the north west of Albert*).

15th At 7 a.m. proceeded to Albert to the late stand & brought back stores etc. The town was again shelled & Taubes over this part during the night. A very fine day. Heavy bombardment by the British & a great attack made, & Beaumont Hamel & St Pierre Division captured. A great achievement by our troops. Arrived back at 2 p.m.

16th A sharp frost during the evening & very cold. We are stationed on a hill top here & it is very bleak. At 9.30 p.m. proceeded to Albert, (4 lorries) to the yard & loaded up with gun-stores etc. A very fine day. About 800 prisoners seen being brought in. Many of our aeroplanes up. Several papers dropped from German machines & these came to earth in & around Albert. A balloon passed over most likely an enemy one, for our airmen attacked it, turning their machine guns on it, which made it descend more rapidly. Arrived back at 4 p.m. Taubes again over during the night. 2 of our antiair-craft (*anti-aircraft*) shells fell in a field near our column & burst. Another sharp frost during the night.

17th All had to run their engines for ¼ hr after the 8.30 p.m. parade, afterwards letting out all the water. Taubes came over at a great height during the morning & dropped several bombs in the Albert district. Heavy bombardment by our guns.

18th Snow fell during the night & a cold wind got up. Too cold to work & very little done. Nothing of any importance occurred.

19th A very wet morning, & again very dirty. Half-holiday given. Several lorries on Engineers Work. Heard that the 9th Division Supply Column (M.T.) had been shelled out of Albert & that they had come back to Franvilliers (*Franvillers*). Noticed a great prisoner's camp had been erected here.

20th Sharp frost during the night. All busy cleaning lorries, as the General of Transports is expected to pay us a visit tomorrow. Heard that a German was over here flying a British machine which they had captured. A German prisoner at Franvilliers (**Franvillers**) shot for refusing to work. (**German Prisoners of War were subject to the harsh British Military discipline after capture, and although executions of German prisoners were not common, they did happen.**)

21st Again very busy & all lorries looked a credit to the men we were informed by our O.C. Given a half-holiday for the General never came. A nice day & our aeroplanes very active. Heavy bombardment on this front by both sides. The S.S. Britannic (Hospital Ship) sunk off the Greek Coast. All lives saved. (**HMHS (His Majesty's Hospital Ship) Britannic was the sister ship of RMS (Royal Mail Ship's) Titanic and Olympic. On 21st November 1916 whist sailing just off the Greek Island of Kea she struck an underwater mine and sank in just under an hour, of the 1,065 people on board only 30 lost their lives.**)

22nd Several lorries on Engineers work. Nothing interesting to note.

23rd A very fine day. 2 new guns arrived at Albert station for our battery. The two right-half guns at Contalmaison position were brought out of action & taken to the Ordanance (**Ordnance**) Workshops. At 2 p.m. I was inoculated by the Corps M.O. & given 48 hrs sick leave. Braemar Castle, (Hospital Ship) sunk off Greek Coast. (**This Hospital ship did strike a mine in the Aegean Sea but unlike HMHS Britannia she didn't sink. The ship was towed to safety, repaired and eventually scrapped in the mid 1920's.**)

24th Very sick & in bed all day. A very cold day & rain at intervals.

25th Heavy rain during the night & this morning. At 3 p.m. packed up & proceeded to the new position for column, on the Avely,-Albert road. A rough place & knee deep in mud. We are about 4 miles from the trenches here &

beside a (*an*) R.F.A. (*Royal Field Artillery*) Amm. (*Ammunition*) Column & just behind our howitzer batteries. On guard for 2 hrs at night.

26th Again much rain. The rest of the column removed from Baizieux to here. Very busy putting up the cookhouse & bivouacs etc. The 40th & 112th Columns arrived here too during the day.

27th A better day, but so damp & cold & impossible to keep dry amongst so much mud. Very busy putting up recreation tent etc. About 6.30 p.m. the Germans commenced to shell Albert station which is about ½ mile away. The 1st shell dropped amongst the horses opposite our lorries, but did not explode. This continued for several hours through the night.

28th Commenced to dig a dug-out & at 11.30 a.m. orders came through we were to move to Warloy-Baillon (*situated about 6 miles to the west of Albert*). Packed all up at once & the column moved off for the above place at once, & all very glad to leave here. The Adjutant & Medical Officer of the Park have both condemned the position.

29th Very busy cleaning up the new park & all men on fatigue. This is a very nice village. The 15th Division, whose H2's are here went into action today. Very foggy & cold.

30th Usual work for day. A concert held in our canteen, by men of the park & it was a great success. Sharp frost during the night. A heavy bombardment at intervals through the night.

1st December 1916 The Durham Light Infantry came in here for a month's rest from the trenches. Very cold & sharp frost at night. Several lorries on Engineers Work. Several men from the Park went on furlough. (*Leave*)

2nd Busy cleaning lorries etc. Unloaded the gun stores off my lorry. Heavy gun fire on this front by both sides. Albert shelled by the Germans.

3rd Usual work for day. Half Holiday given. At 12 noon proceeded to Dernarcourt to Engineers Dump & loaded with trench boards & took same to their advanced dump at Contalmaison. Arrived back at 7 p.m. Very foggy night. Much artillery coming out of action for a rest.

4th Usual work for day. 6 lorries on Engineers Work. My birthday & the usual party & feast at night. Heavy bombardment during the night & enemy aeroplanes over this district.

5th A very wet day. On guard at night for the 34th time. 8 lorries on Engineers Work. Rifle drill at 8.30 a.m.

6th Rifle drill again at 8.30 a.m. At 2 p.m. all the columns stationed here paraded in drill order before the Major, who inspected all & was very pleased with the appearance of his men.

7th At 7.30 a.m. proceeded to Albert station (7 lorries) to cart stones for the R.E. (***Royal Engineers***). Arrived back at 5 p.m. Our guns very active. 2 new guns arrived for the 19th Siege &during the day the enemy shelled our position at Contalmaison very heavily & killed a sergeant & wounded 4 gunners.

8th Usual work for day. The two new guns taken into a position at Bazentin in the morning. A very wet day & nothing much occurred.

9th On Engineers work at Albert & arrived back to 5.30 p.m. Strict orders that no driver to exceed 6 miles per hour with his lorry. Our officer in command commenced a course of lectures in the recreation room. His first subject was on the construction of road. Reported sick at 8 a.m.

10th Usual work on lorries. Half holiday given. A very foggy wet day. 5 lorries on R.E. Work. Paid 10 francs towards our Xmas dinner. Paid 30 francs. 7 geese bought for the dinner.

11th On R.E. Work at Albert Station for the day. The Germans shelled Albert at intervals. Nothing important to note.

12th A very wet day. 5 lorries on R.E. Work. Rum issued at night. The 1st of the season. Heard that Lieu (*Lieutenant*) Farmer who is on leave is at home sick, & not returning at present.

13th On R.E. Work again at Albert station. Our aeroplanes very active as it is a fine clear day. The Germans shelled our trenches heavily during the night.

14th Usual work for day. 2 new Thornycroft lorries attached to our column in exchange for 2 Saurers. All busy on fatigue making a new recreation room, corporals mess etc.

15th On R.E. Work at Albert for the day. Arrived back at 6 p.m. Much artillery coming out of action. A fine day & our airmen very busily engaged. A Taube brought down on this front during the morning.

16th Heard of a great French success at Verdun. 8,000 prisoners & many guns being captured. Renewed activity by the British before Kut in Mesopatamia (*Mesopotamia*). Heavy bombardment by the British on this front.

17th 8 lorries on R.E. Work at Albert. A wet day & the usual half holiday. Lecture at 5 p.m. in the recreation room, the subject being on "bearing of an engine." Much heavy firing on this front during the night.

18th At 6 p.m. proceeded to Vignacourt (4 lorries) to fetch faggots for road making. Took same to the LA Boiselle-Contalmaison Road. Had trouble with the petrol supply. No 6 lorry had a back-wheel come off on returning. Arrived back at park at 1.30 a.m. on the following morning.

19th Usual work on lorry. New water joint fitted. On guard at night for the 35th time, 2 lorries on R.E. Work. All columns paraded before the Major of the Park & he presented the Military Medal to several N.C.O's for bravery on the day of the fire at the H.Q. at Albert.

20th A fine day. Snow during the evening & a sharp frost. On orders that Major Nott had been awarded the D.S.O. & the Adjutant the Military Cross. 1st issue of Green Envelopes whilst been on the Somme front, 6 lorries on R.E. Work.

21st On R.E. Work at Albert station. Arrived back at 6 p.m. The Germans shelled Albert. German prisoners engaged to load the lorries. Officers of the Park sent out on the main roads to trap men driving lorries above the 6 miles per hour limit.

22nd At 6.30 a.m. proceeded to G. Dump & took a load of timber to Fricourt Farm to the Indian Cavalry. Arrived back at 6 p.m. Much artillery coming back for a rest. All were Australian Divisions. Albert again shelled.

23rd A very cold windy day. All busy preparing for Xmas. 6 lorries on R.E. Work. Pte Shaw & Pte Moore appeared before the O.C. for damaging a tube of a radiator. Both deprived 2 days pay.

24th At 6.15 a.m. proceeded to Albert station (6 lorries) on R.E. Work. About 200 lorries from park waited in the station till 1 p.m. & no stone train arrived so all returned. The Band of the 50th Division played Christmas carol's during the night. A terrific bombardment by the British during the night.

25th A general holiday & no lorries out. At 2 p.m. the whole company sat down to a splendid dinner consisting of roast geese, ham, potatoes, cabbage & apple-sauce. Also plum-pudding & stewed figs & custard. Plenty of beer, whiskey, wine & champagne, cigarettes, apples & oranges, & sweets for all. Everyone had a most enjoyable day. The O.C. & Adjutant of the park paid us a visit & wished us the compliments of the season. He also read letters of good wishes from the General of IV Army, (***General Henry Seymour Rawlinson's IV Army sector sustained the most casualties during the Battle of the Somme at Poziers and Thiepval. After the war he was heavily criticised but at the time Field Marshal Haig refused to sack him because it would have been highlighted in the press that the Battle of the Somme was a complete disaster.***) the Brigadier General of the III Corps Heavy Artillery & Major Nott our O.C. (who is on leave.)

26th 6 lorries on R.E. Work. The remainder of men given a holiday. During last night the British carried out a very heavy bombardment on the enemy lines for about an hour. A good christmas (***Christmas***) greeting supposed to be for them. The Postal Serg (***Sergeant***) killed.

27th At 4 a.m. proceeded to Mericourt (***About 40 miles north near Lens***) to Railhead to take 8" gun wheel from there to Ordnance Workshops at Ribemont. Arrived there at 5 a.m. & waited until 3 p.m. before loaded wheel & arrived home at 5 p.m. Many men going on pass from this station. A beautiful day & aeroplanes very busy.

28th The usual lorries on R.E. Work, & no stone arrived. All busy on lorries. Heard a mine, exploded by the British, go up about 7 a.m. It was on the Beaumont-Hamel front. (***This wasn't the famous Hawthorn Ridge Mine that was detonated on 1st July 1916 and signified the start of the Battle of the Somme.***) The Germans shelled Albert during the night & Taubes over dropping bombs.

29th At 6.15 a.m. proceeded to Albert on R.E. Work. Arrived home at 5.30 p.m. Lieu (*Lieutenant*) Young, went on furlough. The Germans attacked on the Hamel front & gained a footing in our trenches but were quickly driven out.

30th A wet day. On guard for the 36th time. During the night Taubes over our lines & Albert bombed. 6 lorries on R.E. Work. 5 lorries went to Bray to remove troops at 4 p.m.

31st The Royal Warwicks, who are resting here, & who were in the trenches at christmas (*Christmas*), celebrated the incoming of the New Year. A busy evening & concerts etc were being held in almost every estaminet. Our artillery again heavily shelled the enemies lines from about 11.50 p.m. to 1.5 a.m. (*possibly 1.50 a.m.*). As the New Year came in this was how the British celebrated it at the front on the Somme. A very wet night.

'1917'

1st January 1917 At 7 a.m. proceeded to Albert on R.E. Work. Arrived back at 2.30 p.m. No stone train arrived. Albert shelled during the evening; but no damage done.

2nd Usual work for the day. At 9.30 p.m. called out to take 10 men, who were proceeding to England on pass to Mericourt Station. Arrived back at 2 a.m. Heavy snow storm during the night.

3rd The 1st fall of snow this year & a very sharp frost. The Warwicks left here for Abbeville to undergo a special course of training & the 1st Australian division (Anzacs) came in to Warloy for a rest. A fine set of men & great company to be amongst. Many of these men saw here, snow for the 1st time in their lives. All busy snowballing & their officers were hotly snowballed whenever they chanced to be on the roads.

4th Again much snow & a sharp frost. 6 lorries went to Plateau Station to cart stores. At 7 a.m. I took to Albert Station a load of empty petrol cans & then reported to III Corps. Q.M.Sjs (*Quartermaster Sergeants*) Stores & conveyed to Railhead (Viviers Mill) several things. Then returned to Park with III Corps. A.P.C. Mails.

5th At 6 a.m. proceeded to Plateau Station to cart road metal. Took 1 load to Combles & the last 2 Hardecourt & then returned to Park. Freezing hard again.

6th Usual work for day. Bitterly cold. At night the guard told off to keep engines running at intervals during the night. This to be carried out until the thaw set in.

7th News to the effect that the British had extended their line on the Somme, taking over several miles of front, to relieve the French. General Birdword (*Birdwood*) (G.O.C.) Australian divisions was here during the afternoon. *(General William Birdwood was a British Army Officer who eventually rose to the rank of Field Marshal in 1925. He is probably most famous for creating and commanding the ANZAC's (Australian and New Zealand Army Corps) in Gallipoli, he was also responsible for planning and accomplishing the very successful evacuation of the Dardanelles Army in December 1915 – January 1916.)*

8th At 7 a.m. proceeded to Corbie (6 lorries) there joined up some 50 others & all loaded with Guardsmen & took a Brigade to Maurepas. Returned to Corbie & picked up another Brigade & took to above place. Returned to Park at 9 p.m. Had my razor stolen out of haversack by one of the men.

9th Still very cold & a keen frost last night. Usual work on lorries. At 9 p.m. took leave party to Mericourt Station; returned to Park at 12 midnight.

10th At 9 a.m. proceeded to Contalmaison (6 lorries) & loaded with kits & gunners of the R.G.A & took same to Mericourt Station. There loaded up with stores for the 48th Siege Battery & took same to Warloy, where the 48th loaded it on to their lorries.

11th Attended to lorry. The 48th Siege Battery left the Park for a new position further north. Several lorries on R.E. work at Thrones Wood. Taubes over here during the afternoon & were shelled by our guns; but got away.

12th

Epilogue

This was the very last entry in Private Frank Sanderson's second of two notebooks:

It seems slightly chilling that he'd only written '12th' as a last remark without an explanation as to what he did on that very day. Why did he suddenly stopped writing? This last entry left me wondering what had happened to Frank on the 12th January 1917. He'd written an entry in his journal every single day of his time in the army, so why would he simply stop recording his daily life on the Western Front, and on that particular day?

Most of the people I've spoken to came to the same conclusion, Frank must have been 'Killed in Action' whilst collecting another load of ammunition from the rail-head or delivering it to the guns. And given the amount of death and destruction that took place on the Western Front, it is a reasonable assumption. But if he was killed then surely someone would have packed up his personal belongings and returned them to his family back in Hull. Because keeping a personal diary was illegal for a soldier during World War One, Frank's note-books would unquestionably have been handed into an Officer and subsequently destroyed. So if that was the case then how did the diaries make it back to Doncaster and into the possession of Stephen Parsons 100 years later? It's possible that the memoirs could have slipped through the net because a friend may have cleared his kit and sympathetically thought that his family might like to read them.

Regardless of my own assumptions, I set about checking how many Frank Sanderson names were on the WW1 British Commonwealth War Graves (CWGC) lists, and in particular any with a date of death that was recorded as 12th January 1917. Frustratingly, there are plenty of Private Frank Sanderson's registered on the CWGC web-site and a large percentage of them came from Hull, some had also served in the Army Service Corps. None of the Dates of Death came anywhere near the 12th January 1917 and so my particular Frank Sanderson wasn't one of them. After spending hours, unsuccessfully, combing through plenty of archival documents, I eventually dismissed the 'Killed in Action' theory.

One of the male helpers down at the National Archives in Kew rather incredibly came up with his own hypothesis. With an apathetic look on his face he annoyingly offered, "Maybe he just got bored with writing them." I angrily discounted this stupid offering out of hand because most avid diary writers don't just stop writing for no reason. Please note that every other official I dealt with down at Kew, either on the telephone or face to face, were very professional, polite, and incredibly helpful.

The German Luftwaffe of the Second World War weren't very helpful either. In September 1940 Generalfeldmarschall Göering sent over a few of his Heinkel bomber's to deliberately hamper my endeavour's to write a finale for this book. One particular Luftwaffe bomb hit the National Archives and caused a fire which destroyed many documents relating to the First World War, and the service records of Private Frank Sanderson were part of that collateral damage. However, many other military records weren't demolished and so I purchased copies of the Official Unit War Diaries of 282 Company Army Service Corps, 15th Brigade Ammunition Column and both 13th and 19th Siege Batteries. With a little bit of luck Frank might have been mentioned in at least one of these unit war diaries. As a First World War buff, each of these documents were an absolute joy to read and I eagerly scoured them with relish. A lot of the minutes in the documents were mundane though and referred to things like the weather conditions on a particular day, but others contained some fascinating facts like the names of soldiers that had been killed and gallantry awards that had been won, in some cases also briefly describing why the awards were recommended. I read these official war diaries in anticipation of finding the name Private Frank Sanderson ASC and what had happened to him.

Another major problem I had was that I didn't have any information about Frank's early life in Hull, who his family were and what he did for a living before enlisting into the British Army. All I had to go on was the name Frank Sanderson and that his birthday was on the 4th of December, I didn't even know in which year he was born. Stephen Parsons knew very little about his Step-Grandfather and there were no other living relatives who could help fill in the blanks.

I telephoned my friend Colin Booth who works as a volunteer researcher at the Carnegie Heritage Centre in Hull. Like Stevie Johnson in my introduction to this book, Colin was an extraordinary and well respected army boxer who had also served in both the Royal Corps of Transport and the Special Air Service. After one quick phone call Colin invited me to the heritage centre to see if he could be of any help in finding some details about a Frank Sanderson from Hull who was born on the 4th of December. I left Colin with the small amount of information I had and he set about unearthing the evidence I needed. Colin telephoned me a week later and asked me to come and see him at the Carnegie Heritage Centre in Hull, he'd dug out some significant information for me.

Frank Sanderson was born on the 4th of December 1894 and was the second eldest child to Ann Elizabeth Sanderson. According to the 1901 National Census, Ann was a 31 year old widow and the family of five were living in Wellington Lane in Hull. Ann's occupation is registered as having her own means but in the 1911 Census she was re-married to Thomas Coggin who was a General Labourer and 13 years older than her. Thomas and Ann had two further children and they all lived in Harcourt Terrace in Sculcoates. Frank's occupation at the age of 17 is listed as a Leaded Light Maker.

We know from Frank's Diaries that he eventually enlisted into the army on the 23rd of April 1915 and he recorded the most memorable and important incidents of his life over the next 624 days. He'd recorded everything except what had happened to him on the 12th of January 1917. My friend Colin had also discovered on the 1939 Register that Frank married a lady called Gertrude who was both an unpaid domestic and a shop worker, Frank is listed on the same document as a Tea Merchant. The 1939 Register confirmed that Frank hadn't been killed on the 12th of January 1917 because he and Gertrude had had a son whilst living at Walmsley Street in Hull. They named their only child Stanley Oswald Sanderson who was born on the 11th of April 1920. On Stanley's Birth Certificate Frank's profession is recorded as 'Grocers Motor Driver - Ex-Army'. Other than these details we know very little about Frank and Gertrude except that they eventually moved from Hull to Doncaster after the 1939 Register had been recorded. Frank may have moved because of his work or he conceivably thought Doncaster would be a safer place for his family to live. Let's face it, the Luftwaffe certainly gave Hull a pasting between the years of 1939 and 1945.

At the age of 19, Stanley Sanderson was listed on the Register as being an Apprentice Joiner and he was still living at home with Frank and Gertrude on Eastfield Road in Hull; this was just before he enlisted into the Royal Engineers at the start of World War Two. Stanley obviously had the same sense of duty and patriotism as his dad Frank because he served throughout the Second World War and gained a few gongs as he soldiered along. Stanley was awarded a Military Medal 'FOR BRAVERY IN THE FIELD', the Africa Star with an 8th Army Clasp, the Italy Star, the Defence Medal, and the War Medal which has a Mentioned in Despatches Oak Leaf on the ribbon. The Oak Leaf is another award for an act of gallantry in the face of the enemy.

Years after the war Stanley became the Clerk of Works at RAF Lindholme which is where he met a young Steve Parsons, at the time Steve was working as a plumber for MPBW (Ministry of Public Building and Works). As a consequence Stanley eventually met Steve's widowed mum Audrey and they fell in love, in the course of time Stanley and Audrey got married. Steve fondly remembers Stanley and describes the very brave ex-soldier as a quiet and dignified man who was very gentlemanly. Stanley's father Frank Sanderson died of cancer on the 18th of February 1958 at the age of 64. His wife Gertrude Annie Sanderson lived on until the 28th of September 1981. When Stanley died he passed on his and Frank's medals to Audrey, he also passed on his dads diaries from the First World War and after Audrey died they were all bequeathed to Steve Parsons. So, that's how the diaries ended up back in Doncaster and were eventually passed onto Steve Parsons after the death of his mum. What, though, happened to Frank in Albert on the 12th of January 1917 and why did he simply stop making daily entries in his journals?

If this was a Hollywood Film then a third dairy would be found somewhere and all the answers you want to hear would be provided, or maybe the director of the film would send a team of researchers down to the National Archives and they would dig out the story they needed. Unfortunately life isn't like that, there are no surviving family members or comrades who can tell us exactly what happened on that day early in 1917. The last surviving veterans of the Great War, like Harry Patch and Henry Allingham, died nearly a decade ago. Even though the records at the National Archives are still today being re-examined and digitally recorded for future reference, they are erratic to say the least. The reasons for this are mainly because of the way the papers were written, recorded, and filed at the time, and not forgetting of course the damage caused by Herman Göering and his mates.

All we do know is that Frank was more than likely wounded, gassed or became ill in one form or another. Even if we don't know the exact details, we do know that he survived as a soldier of the Great War and had a son who proved to be an exceptional soldier and an all-round great man. To give you some idea of how Frank's supposed wounding may have been recorded in an Official War Diary, without mentioning his name, the following are just some of the reports I've read:

1. The work at this time was very dangerous and hard, the battery Major, other officers and a number of men killed. Only four of the ASC column drivers were wounded and the Daimler car wrecked by shellfire.

2. One lorry destroyed by shellfire, three ASC men killed and four wounded.

3. ASC other rank casualties, 4 killed 6 wounded.

4. During this work 3 ASC men were killed and three others wounded.

5. 2 Lorries destroyed by fire after shell burst. 1 x ASC soldier killed and 1 wounded.

6. Capt (*Captain*) Mellish reported at 10.30 a.m. that 2 men (Sergt (*Sergeant*) Reynold and another man) had been found dead in the store lorry. The men were evidently suffocated by fumes from an asetilyne (*acetylene*) lamp. The body of the lorry is wood and doors and windows were found closed.

7. The OC 12th A.S.P. reported to me at 3 p.m. That 2 of his lorries had been destroyed by fire owing to a shell bursting alongside them and that one ASC man had been killed and one wounded. I went off at once to see the lorries or what was left of them. The lorries were on the road just by Annequin Village.

8. Authors note: I refer you, the reader, to the story about two ASC soldiers killed by a train at the top of page 58.

Although we don't know the full story about M2/081329 Private Frank Sanderson of 282 Company ASC, he was obviously much luckier than the 72,246 other soldiers whose names are recorded on the Thiepval War Memorial near Albert. Those soldiers were killed in action during the Battle of the Somme at the same time Frank was serving in the same area, the soldiers recorded on the Thiepval Memorial have no known grave and their story will never be known. At least Frank got to come home with his diaries and you the reader can pass on his tales.

Brian (Harry) Clacy

A very dapper Stanley Sanderson presenting a prize at his local working men's club (circa 1960's).

Stanley Sanderson's World War Two Medals

Left to Right: The Military Medal. The 1939-1945 Star. The Africa Star with 8th Army Clasp. The Italy Star. The Defence Medal. The War Medal with a Mentioned In Despatches Oak Leaf.

Army Form W. 3121 recommending Corporal Stanley Sanderson RE for an award of the Military Medal. Note: Counter signed by General Bernard Law Montgomery who was Commander of the Eighth Army 'Desert Rats' in 1943. Other notable signatures are the C in C of Middle East Forces General Sir Henry Maitland Wilson, the Commander of 30 Corps Lieutenant General Sir Oliver Leese, and Commander of 7 Armoured Division Major General Raymond Briggs.

This is how the London Gazette of 4 May 1943 published the award:

Recommendation for Award for Sanderson, Stanley Oswald. Rank: Corporal. Service No: 2020368. Regiment: Royal Engineers.

This NCO was i/c (*in command*) party of R.E. (*Royal Engineers*) attached to C Sqn 12th Royal Lancers from ZAUIA to ZUARA.

He many times by hard work and determination, quickly found mines and filled in demolitions.

At SABRATHA he was right up in front and filled in the A.T. (*Anti-Tank*) ditch under fire, enabling our troops to advance. On the same day, when filling in a demolition, he was wounded by machine-gun fire on the open road. The next day, in spite of his wound's, Sgt (*Sergeant*) Sanderson was again "on the job", and his devotion to duty was an example to all.

Signed by: B. L. Montgomery. GOC Eighth Army.

BUCKINGHAM PALACE.

I greatly regret that I am
unable to give you personally the
award which you have so well earned.
I now send it to you with
my congratulations and my best
wishes for your future happiness.

George R.I.

2020368 L/Sjt. S.O. Sanderson, M.M.,

Corps of Royal Engineers.

Stanley Sanderson's Military Medal Certificate
signed by King George VI.

By the KING'S Order the name of
Lance-Sergeant S. O. Sanderson, M.M.,
Royal Engineers
was published in the London Gazette on
13 January, 1944.
as mentioned in a Despatch for distinguished service.
I am charged to record
His Majesty's high appreciation.

Secretary of State for War

Stanley Sanderson's Mentioned in Despatches Oak
Leaf Certificate signed by Sir P J Grigg, Secretary of
State for War from February 1942 until July 1945.

Private Frank Sanderson's First World War medals. Commonly referred to as 'Pip' 'Squeak' and 'Wilfred' by most World War One Veterans.

Frank's headstone at St Wilfrids Church in Cantley Doncaster.

The author, Steve and Eileen Parsons, Nicky Clacy and Terry Cavender.

Steve Parsons at his Step-Grandfathers headstone.

Bibliography

Army Service Corps 1902 – 1918. Michael Young. LEO COOPER 2000 an imprint of Pen & Sword Books Ltd.

Wait for the Wagon (The Story of the Royal Corps of Transport and its predecessors 1794-1993. Edited by John Sutton. LEO COOPER 1998 an imprint of Pen & Sword Books Ltd.

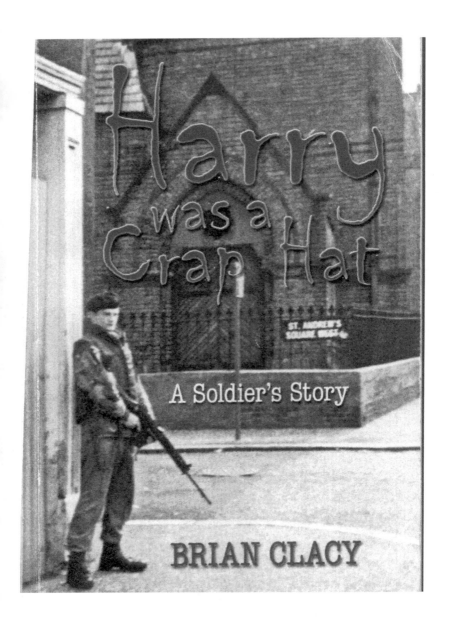

Harry was a Crap Hat

A Soldier's Story

BRIAN CLACY

TWO MEDICS, ONE NURSE AND A GOB DOCTOR

Two wars in Iraq without fighting

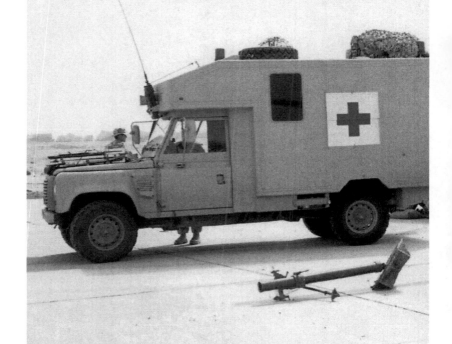

Brian (Harry) Clacy

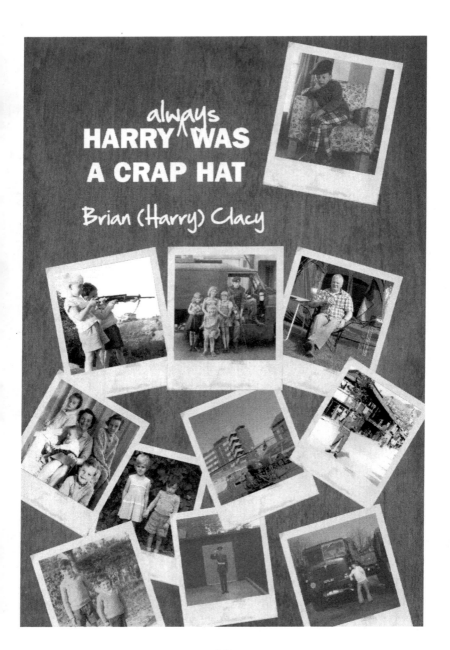

HARRY always WAS
A CRAP HAT

Brian (Harry) Clacy

RICKSHAWS, CAMELS AND TAXIS

Rogues, Ruffians and Officers of the
Royal Corps of Transport

Written by **Brian (Harry) Clacy**

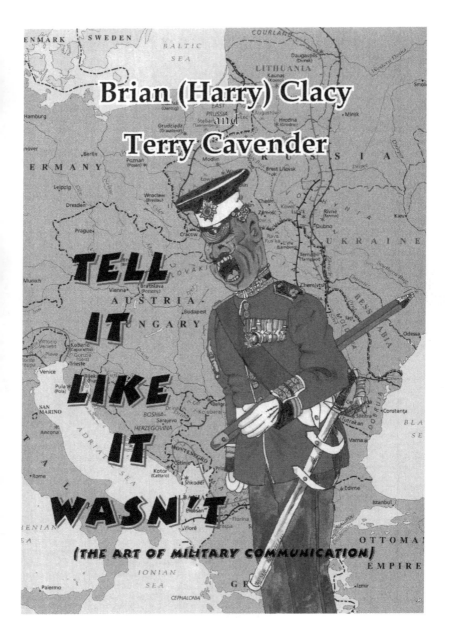

Brian (Harry) Clacy
and
Terry Cavender

TELL
IT
LIKE
IT
WASN'T

(THE ART OF MILITARY COMMUNICATION)